DEDICATION

This book is dedicated to the memory of my
beloved parents, Mr. Rufus Burgest, Sr., whose
character serves as a model for my life and to my
beloved mother, Mrs. Marie (Cooper) Burgest, who
passed away during my early childhood. I cherish
the memories of her, which relatives and friends
have shared with me.

ACKNOWLEDGEMENTS

First, I will acknowledge Mrs. Hortense Cochrane, Professor Emeritus of Syracuse University, who has been a source of encouragement for me throughout my professional development, and Dr. William P. Sapp, Sr. and Dr. C. Wayman Alston, two of my senior colleagues, who helped "show me the way" when I was a young professional. Further, I acknowledge Rev. Junius Dudley, who helped me to appreciate the "ministry of love" in my teaching and work with individuals.

The following persons were helpful in the preparation of this manuscript by reading and providing critical feedback: Mr. Henry Reid, a social work pioneer of Chicago; Dr. Sonya Monroe-Clay, Dr. Prince McLemore, Dr. Ana Kong and Dr. June O. Patton of Governors State University; Dr. Phillip M. Mbhiti of the University of Nairobi in Nairobi, Kenya (East Africa) and Mr. Michael Anderes, a professional social worker in mental health.

Many thanks and appreciations of love must go to Loretta, my wife, and my children, Juanita Marie, Angela Lynore, David Raymond II and Paul Reginald. This task could not have been accomplished without their inspiration, love and spiritual support.

In conclusion, I must acknowledge a few of the individuals who played a major role in the typing and editing of this manuscript. They are Mrs. Beverly Fortson, Ms. Lillie Conrad, Mrs. Gladys Cochrane, Ms. Amelia L. Taylor, Mrs. Sophia Wanjiru and Mrs. Pamela Zener; and for the final manuscript done through the "magic" of word processing, Ms. Jan Gray and Ms. Barbara Degnan of Professional Support Systems. Special thanks to Ms. Helen Hudson at the University Press of America for her patience.

TABLE OF CONTENTS

PREFACE

The major focus of this manuscript will be on social casework intervention with Third World minorities in America who are generally referred to as People of Color. The concept People of Color will be used interchangeably in this manuscript with the terminology Third World minorities in America. Third World minorities include Native Americans, Black Americans, Puerto Ricans and Mexican-Americans, with a minor emphasis on Chinese-Americans, Koreans and Japanese-Americans.

The dynamic that gave birth to the need for a resource of this type has its impetus in the explosion of ethnic and racial consciousness and dignity among Third World minorities that was first ignited in the middle 1960's by Black Americans. The social work profession and, specifically, the social casework discipline were suddenly confronted with overt manifestation of ethnic and racial pride and respect among the Third World minority clientele. The acceptance and manifestation of these new cultural values by People of Color began reshaping educational and practice skill orientations in social work. Previously, the social casework discipline functioned under the premise of "colorblindness" by denying the importance and relevance of race and ethnicity in the worker/client relationship. However, the social casework discipline was required to reorganize its orientation in the late 60's in order to encompass the unique cultural realities manifested by individuals of the Third World ethnic and racial groups.

One of the significant efforts utilized by the social work professional organizations, educational institutions, associations and social agencies was the recruitment of minority educators, practitioners and students into their system. The view held by these organizations was that the presence of Third World minority workers would provide more relevant casework services to minority clients.

Secondly, there were attempts and efforts by the
profession to create ethnic literature and design
the social work curriculum to reflect the unique
culture and way of life of Third World minorities. Thirdly, there were the creations of
numerous conferences, workshops and institutes to
assist in preparing those in the social casework
discipline for effective casework practice in the
Third World communities. In addition to the
above, there were human relation labs, sensitivity and insight into inter-personal growth
among members of the majority culture with
members of the Third World racial and ethnic
groups. One of the culminating activities of the
social work professional associations with
auxiliary publishing firms was the solicitation
of materials relating to Third World clients,
devoting several volumes of the social work journals to themes specific to Third World minorities. Nevertheless, praciticioners, educators and
students must continue to randomly search through
journals and conference proceedings and synthe-
size literature on Third World minorities. At
present, there is no original book available that
addresses social casework with Third World
minorities.

The efforts and actions by social work educators,
scholars, practitioners and publishing firms to
create a multi-cultural and racial curriculum
have not resulted in one original book. The
purpose of this manuscript is to fill that void
and provide the necessary synthesis and clarity.
The primary target of concern in this text is
People of Color in the United States. However,
this book has implications for People of Color all
over the world because the minorities described
in this manuscript are indigenous to cultures
from all parts of the world.

In conclusion, this book is not designed to
instruct a particular racial/ethnic group member
on how to be effective with another racial/ethnic

group member. This book is designed to provide a process whereby workers of both the majority and minority cultures in America will learn how to become effective with clients in each different culture, while at the same time learn how to become increasingly effective with members of the same culture.

Please note that the pseudonyms used in many of the case illustrations from professinal literature have been changed in order to provide for chronological consistency in this book.

INTRODUCTION

In terms of skin color, humans may be divided into two distinct groupings consisting of the darker complexioned people of the world or "People of Color," as they are traditionally referred, and the white complexioned people of the world. Anthropologists have divided humans into basically three distinctive racial groupings: (1) Caucasoid, (Europeans/white), (2) Negroid (African/Blacks) and Mongoloids (Asians/yellow). Caucasians consist primarily of European whites who are light complexioned individuals with straight hair. The Negroid race is characterized by having a dark complexioned skin, flat nose, thick lips and wooly hair. The Mongoloids are tan to dark in complexion with straight black hair and, usually, slanting eyes. Humans have also been divided along philosophical and ideological perspectives: the Western epistemological world view and the Eastern epistemological world view. These world views are not restricted to specific geographical locations in the hemisphere but refer to a commonality and uniqueness in a thought and way of life expressed by a people across geographical boundaries. The only commonality that appears to exist between the East and West is that the Colored people of the world fall in the category of the Eastern world view and the white people of the world fall within the category of the Western epistemological world view. In addition, the Colored people of the world generally make up the Third World societies.

Culture is the sum total of a people's way of life, including beliefs, art, morals, laws, customs and rituals transmitted from one generation to another and binding people together collectively. Ethnicity may be defined as a heterogenous population of people who are of the same or different nationalities/races but bound together by a common history, geography, customs and way of life. In the epistemological world view, there is consensus that humans are divided

into the Eastern philosophical world view and the
Western philosophical world view. Epistemology
may be defined as the origin and etiology of
thought and logic giving birth to one's conception of oneself, others, one's surroundings and
one's relationship with God. There are those who
are quick to imply that such a description denotes culture. However, there is a causal relationship between world view and culture in the
same way there is a causal relationship between
language and culture. The causal relationship
between world view and culture does not suggest
which influences the other, for either may be the
causal agent, both may be effects of a common
cause, or there may be a mutual causal action.
But, the fact remains that there is a definite
indispensable correlation between world view and
culture.

"Third World" in contemporary society has become
synonymous with "underdeveloped" nations of the
world, such as those found in Africa, Asia and
South America. The operational definition of
Third World minorities in this manuscript refers
to ethnic and racial groupings whose genetic
origins are Negroid or Mongoloid and who are
located in America. More specifically, America's
Third World minorities refer to individuals and
groups whose origin is identified with nations
defined as Third World but who are now living in
America. If we explore further, we will find
that the Eastern world view is made up mostly of
societies considered to be of the Third World.

As we come to understand the basic relationship
between race, ethnicity, culture and Third World,
it is also important to understand the fundamental description and function of social casework
and its relevance to Third World minorities in
America. Social casework is a method of social
work practice in the same way that group work,
community organization and administration is a
method of social work practice. Social casework
is specifically designed to help and assist individuals find solutions to psychological and

social adjustment problems that they are unable to handle satisfactorily through their own efforts.

Social casework practitioners are taught to utilize the strengths of the individual and his/her capacity to develop and adjust in a way that will bring him/her satisfaction. Social caseworkers help individuals by primarily using the tools of listening, developing rapport and establishing a consciously developed relationship with the art and skills of human relations. The foundation of the caseworkers' knowledge-base is rooted in understanding human behavior, self-insight, sensitivity and awareness of the values in self that may prohibit the therapeutic gathering of the facts concerning the case as well as a diagnosis and projected treatment plans.

The classical description of the function and practice of social casework provided above presents the ideal model, dimensions and parameters without any specific regard to the dilemma and difficulties related to race and culture.

One of the primary purposes of this text is to address the specific concerns and dynamics of race and culture as it may pertain to People of Color in America. A few of the basic competencies that the reader may derive from this text to fulfill the ideal dimensions of social. casework are listed below. The competency statements are divided into **cognitive** (knowledge) or behavioral objectives, which stipulate the precise skills that one will be able to obtain from the content. The other competency statements are under the **affective** (attitudinal) category, which stipulate self-insight and self-awareness skills.

Cognitive Skills (Knowledge)

Identify and analyze the implication and relevance of the principles and ethics of social casework practice with Third World minorities in

America.

Identify and analyze professional case recordings of worker/client relationship with Third World minorities in America to evaluate and assess the effectiveness and ineffectiveness of the techniques and strategies.

Identify and analyze the theoretical base for the unique culture of Third World minorities and specific intervention skills needed.

Identify and analyze the unique variables in race and ethnicity that may prohibit the development of casework intervention skills.

Trace, analyze and evaluate the historical developments and dynamics of social casework with People of Color.

Identify and analyze the dynamics that may prohibit an effective casework relationship between members of the same and different racial/ethnic groups.

Identify and analyze the deficits and strengths inherent in social casework practice and theory as it may pertain to Peple of Color.

Identify the similarities and commonalities in Third World minority cultures and their implication for social casework practice.

Affective Skills (Attitudinal)

Increase awareness and sensitivity to the ethnic/ racial and cultural uniqueness of all Third World minorities in America.

Increase sensitivity and self-awareness regarding one's own ethnic/racial and cultural identity.

Increase self-insight and sensitivity into the negative stereotypes, assumptions and prejudices

relevance of such dynamics for social casework with People of Color.

Chapter III: Social Casework Intervention:
                White Worker/Black Client and
                Black Worker/White Client
                Relationship

Social casework practice with People of Color in America began primarily with Black Americans. At first, the Black American was a recipient of casework services offered by white institutions, but later, many Blacks became caseworkers with white clients as well as Black clients.

Therefore, this chapter is provided to define and analyze the psychodynamics of the casework relationship between the white worker/Black client; Black worker/white client, and Black worker/Black client relationship with implications for the white worker/white client relationship.

Chapter IV: Social Casework Intervention:
                (Native Americans/Puerto Ricans/
                Mexican-Americans/Selected
                Orientals)

In this chapter the primary objective is to define, identify and analyze the dynamics of the relationship between the unique culture of these ethnic cultures and the implications for social casework intervention.

Chapter V: Some Critical Comments of Social
                Study: Diagnosis: Theory

In the final chapter of this book the primary objective is to analyze and critically evaluate the social work theory base as it pertains to social study, investigation and social diagnosis of People of Color in America.

Chapter I.

PRINCIPLES OF THE CASEWORK RELATIONSHIP

In all of the academic professions that are involved in the delivery of services, such as
Medicine, Law, Psychiatry and Social Work, there
is the existence of a philosophical and ideological preamble of ideals defined as principles,
oaths, creeds or codes of ethics governing the
interaction and relationship between the con-
sumers of services and the worker. In the profession of social work there are two components:
there is a code of ethics that itemizes the
statements of belief and moral conduct and the
principles of the casework relationship that provide the fundamental frame of reference for the
attitudes, values and judgments that workers must
internalize and manifest in their relationship
with clients. In this chapter, we will focus on
the principles of the casework relationship as
they relate to People of Color in America.

Principles, creeds and codes of ethics are
usually by-products of the profession in that
they emerge from the inherent practicing ideology
and philosophy of the profession rather than
being superimposed by a collection of thinkers at
the beginning of the profession. It is natural
and purposeful that Felix Biestek, author of
Casework Relationship, identified the specific
concepts of the principles decades after social
casework practice was developed.

The seven principles of the casework relationship
as composed and defined by Felix Biestek became
assimilated and adopted by the social work profession as the definitive statement to govern the
casework relationship. It may appear on first
thought that there is no need to elaborate on the
seven principles of the casework relationship as
they might relate to People of Color in America.
There may also be the assumption that the

1

principles of the casework relatinship as stipulated by Biestek transcend both race and ethnicity and that the generic nature of the principles
should be applicable to all individuals regard-
less of race or culture. Nonetheless, the historical experiences in social work practice and
education with Third World minorities in America
have demonstrated that the social theory, methods
and techniques implemented without specific regard to race and culture have proven ineffective
and inadequate. As one source puts it:

> Schools of social work have, for the
> most part, been oblivious to the need
> for adapting methods of practice to
> minority groups. Rather, they teach
> practice derived from a generic method
> that is dictated primarily by the ma-
> jority. Yet, much social work practice
> is carried out in the United States
> with minority groups and, too often,
> social workers apply it by a blanket
> method supposedly effective with all
> people. Each minority group has its
> own problems and personality -- derived
> from long-existing cultural and moral
> values, language patterns of behavior,
> socio-economic conditions, ethnic back-
> ground, and many other factors. Social
> work practice in a minority community
> shows that besides the variations that
> must be made in the generic method to
> suit individuals, certain adaptations
> should be made in applying social work
> methods to the specific minority
> group.[1]

One of the most blatant pitfalls in the generic
application of social theory and method in social
work practice has been the use of the "color-
blindness"[2] approach by social caseworkers in
working with clients from different racial
groups. The "colorblindness" approach is a simple disregard of the relevance of color and ethnicity in the worker/client relationship. Sec-

ondly, social caseworkers have operated under the assumption that the white middle-class standards were a universal guide to define, analyze and diagnose the behavior of all clients. Therefore, such terms as "culturally deprived," "culturally disadvantaged" and "culturally under-privileged"[3] were created.

Thus, it is necessary that specific elaborations, evaluations and dramatizations of the seven principles of the casework relationship become highlighted in relationship to People of Color. Too often, as described above, the unique dimensions inherent in the worker/client relationship with Third World minority clients are obscured in the generic application.

In introducing the seven principles of the casework relationship and their relationship to People of Color, it is important, first of all, to identify a few of the basic similarities and commonalities existing in the cultural experiences of People of Color in the United States. All of the principles of the casework relationship must be viewed with the following commonalities existing among Third World minority cultures. The similarities and commonalities are as follows:

> Victimized by negative cultural stereotypes associated with blackness and darkness.

> Intense bitterness and conflict with majority race as reflected in the history of oppression, colonization and/or slavery.

> Experience of conflict with external society due to unique customs and ways.

> Distrust and suspicion in negotiations with majority systems and individuals.

> Strong feelings of in-group racial/

3

ethnic solidarity, pride and dignity.

Anti-white hostility and aggression due to discrimination, prejudices and oppression.

Seven Principles of the Casework Relationship

INDIVIDUALIZATION

This principle is defined as "the recognition and understanding of each client's unique qualities-...based upon the right of human beings to be individuals and to be treated not just as a human, but **this** human being with his personal difference."[4]

Individualization in the worker/client relationships with People of Color, first and foremost, requires that the factors of race and ethnicity must be recognized as being of primary importance. During interactions with People of Color the emphasis of the social casework relationship should be on **this particular** human being, taking under consideration the **race, ethnicity** and unique cultural qualities of the individual. The traditional social work practice approach of denying race and ethnicity as being relevant in the casework process has specifically impeded the casework relationship between white workers and Black clients.

The underlying assumption inherent in the "color-blindness" premise has been that consideration of race, color and ethnicity of the client in the worker/client relationship may somehow undermine the factors of **individualization** in that the recognition of race and ethnicity of a client by the worker may create prejudices in the worker. The overriding assumption of the social casework discipline has been that the element of "humanness" or "being human" is separated from race, ethnicity and color. Therefore, the accepted view of the social casework profession has been to simply look at a client as a client and a human being as just a human being without regard for the race and ethnicity of the client.

In regard to People of Color, the traditional interpretation of **individualization** provides social workers with a ready-made escape for making allowances for the effects of discriminatory practices and personal prejudices by obliterating any differences between being "colored" and being "human." Moreover, social caseworkers may be prohibited from developing self-insight by denying prejudices and racism in self under the camouflage of not recognizing race and ethnicity. Implicit in the America culture is a series of negative stereotypes and myths regarding Third World cultures, and the denial of color by the worker may indicate an acceptance of these negative myths and stereotypes. The denial of color and ethnicity may provide an opportunity for the worker to maintain the negative myths and stereotypes associated with color and ethnicity. If color is considered relevant in the worker/client relationship, then the worker would be persuaded to confront his/her own internalized myths and stereotypes associated with color, race and ethnicity.

Perhaps the most destructive manifestation of individualization with People of Color is the attempt of the worker to separate the race and ethnicity of a client from his/her "humanness." This approach may be seen as a blatant indication of prejudice and racism practiced by the professional in that it suggests that the social worker could not justifiably view a minority client as "human" unless the factors of ethnicity and race were removed. It might be said that white/whiteness and white people are the epitomy of that which is "human," while Third World minorities (People of Color) are the epitomy of that which is "nonhuman." The educational training in social work has traditionally made it possible, through the denial of race and ethnicity, for social caseworkers to justify their relationship with minority clients by unconsciously assigning them the status of being "white" in the "color-blindness" approach.

Obstacles Presented and the Role of the Worker

Do away with the "colorblindness" tradition and recognize the color, race and ethnicity of the client as important and relevant factors in the worker/client relationship.

The social work profession must sensitize workers to the factor that race and ethnicity are important and crucial concerns to consider in the professional relationship with People of Color. It has been stated earlier that: (1) traditionally, those in the social work profession accepted the view that color and race are unimportant and should be disregarded and overlooked in the relationship with Third World minorities, (2) during the early sixties social work educators and scholars began to challenge the "colorblindness" approach of "a client is a client" and racial identity should not be taken under consideration. It was further pointed out that (3) recognition of color implies that some unsound practice has taken place, and (4) the thinking of the sixties and seventies by the social work profession and social work scholars should have revolutionized the thinking and approaches of casework practitioners in this regard.

Modern day critics on the "unimportance" of race and ethnicity in the **individualization** process must readily accede to the fact that the failure to recognize the most obvious would truly render the caseworker helpless in recognizing the more subtle problems that the client may bring. A basic contradiction in individualization and social casework practice has been the use of culture as a relevant factor, but the avoidance and nonrecognition of race and ethnicity. Yet, race and ethnicity must be associated as an integral

6

part of culture.

Do away with the negative myths and stereotypes regarding race, ethnicity and color.

In the American society there is an accumulation of negative myths and stereotypes regarding various ethnic and racial groups. One of the key inhibiting factors of the negative myths and stereotypes perpetuated is that they may prohibit the worker from looking at factors in self that may block the development of an effective relationship with clients. This principle applies to workers and clients of the same and different racial and ethnic groups in that any worker may see a "client as a client" disregarding ethnicity and race. In an effort to abolish the negative myths and stereotypes regarding People of Color that affect the individualization process, the worker must:

> Identify and analyze the negative myths and stereotypes existing in the American culture that may block the development of authentic and effective professional relationships with clients of the same and/or different racial/ethnic groups.

> Identify positive myths and assumptions existing in the American culture regarding People of Color and analyze their impact on the social caseworkers' attitude toward self and the minority client.

> Define and identify the positive assumptions needed to facilitate the development of an authentic and effective relationship with a client of the same and/or different ethnic minority.

> Explore, recognize and identify the assumptions, behavior and prejudices in self that may block the development of

7

effective social casework relationship with members of the same and/or different ethnic groups.

Explore, recognize and identify the behavior and attitude needed to facilitate an effective, authentic professional relationship with members of the same and/or different ethnic groups.

Do away with the social work jargon and cliches regarding Third World minorities that mitigate the development of authentic interpersonal professional relationships.

The stereotypical language, cliches and social work jargon used to define and describe Blacks, Puerto Ricans, Mexican-Americans and others are interwebbed within the socialization of the negative myths and stereotypes regarding People of Color in America. Such concepts reflected in social work literature and diagnostic recordings as "culturally deprived," "culturally disadvantaged," "hard-to-reach," "hard-core," "underdeveloped" and "cultural lag" are available masks for social casework practitioners who may wish to use a shield that prohibits self-inventory and self-insight. The end results are that the ineffectiveness in therapy is blamed on the client and that such social work jargon justifies the misconception.

The practitioner may not see the Black or Puerto Rican client as an individual with unique qualities and characteristics; rather, they may only see the symbols hidden behind such concepts as "culturally deprived." Consequently, the caseworker has a built-in escape to avoid the factors in self that may be debilitating in the casework relationship with Third World clients. The caseworker may be unable to see the strengths of the client, which is a necessary step in affecting change. Rather, he/she is limited by the symbols in the social work jargon. Hence, there is also the self-fulfilling prophesy of legitimizing the perceptions inherent in the language. As one social work theorist says, the process of relationship building and **individualization** greatly depends on emotional understanding with reciprocity and rapport being crucial; however, "current cliches can be as handicapping to understanding as were past stereotypes."[5] As we summarize the principles of individualization, the following assumptions will provide the foundation and frame of reference for social work practitioners to follow:

> All People of Color are victims of racism whether they have personally experienced racism or not.

> Racism/white supremacy and in-group classism/elitism have implications for all worker/client relationships.

> The ingrained values of non-Black superiority and Black inferiority in the American society have negative implications for the majority/minority worker/client relationship as well as the minority worker/client relationships.

> Viewing racial, ethnic and cultural uniqueness as being merely different rather than inferior or superior.

> Worker over-identification and overcompensation with client due to negative stereotypes and myths regarding race, ethnicity and culture should be avoided.

ACCEPTANCE

Biestek defines **acceptance** as:

> A principle of action wherein the caseworker perceives and deals with the client as he really is, including his

9

strengths and weaknesses; his congenial
and uncongenial qualities; his positive
and negative feelings; his constructive
and destructive attitudes and behavior,
maintaining all the while a sense of
the client's innate dignity and personal worth.[6]

One of the most devastating, yet unique, qualities inherent in the principle of **acceptance** with
Third World minorities in America is the workers'
attachment of negative assumptions of inferiority
to the life styles and culture of Third World
clients and the corresponding attachment of positive assumptions and superiority to white culture
and life styles. Daniels and Kitano[7] point out
that there is a two-track system composed of non-
white inferiority and white superiority that
dominates the American society as much as the
Protestant Ethic. This two-track system is seen
as ingrained in the American tradition as "red,
white and blue." Therefore, it may be difficult
for a caseworker to perceive Third World clients
as having any constructive and positive attitudes
and behaviors, congenial qualities or a positive
and constructive disposition. In other words,
there may be impediments to the worker meeting
the primary mandate of **acceptance**, which is to
"see the client as he/she really is." This is
particularly crucial when all of the qualities of
acceptance, such as congenial/non-congenial,
constructive/destructive and other attributes,
are contaminated by the worker's negative vision
of Third World cultures.

It may be easy for a worker to implement the
principle of **acceptance** by encouraging the uncongenial and destructive attitudes of a client as
long as the negative disposition is directed away
from the worker. But, difficulties may arise
when those negative qualities and feelings of a
minority client are directed toward the worker.
The negative attitudes and behaviors of a minority client directed toward the worker and the
therapeutic relationship may create insecurities

and discomfort in the worker. The worker may be unable to deal with the client "as he/she really is."

In working with People of Color it may be important to note that feelings of guilt and remorse may develop because the worker may feel that he/she is somehow directly or indirectly responsible for the societal conditions impeding the client. Many majority and minority workers may feel responsible for the client's condition because they are a member of the privileged group in the society and fear that they may be benefiting at the expense of those who are less fortunate.

Given the cross-cultural commonality of race and ethnicity, the worker's experiences may be too closely related to the experiences of the client, or the experiences verbalized by the client may be too painful for the worker to empathize. If the worker has unresolved difficulties in the same area of his/her life as the client, the task of therapy may present problems. Above all, workers of all races and ethnic groups may be victims of the "self-fulfilling prophesy" syndrome. They may perceive only that which they have been socialized through the greater American society to see. Therefore, they can not appropriately assess the strength/weaknesses, positive/negative, constructive/destructive and congenial/uncongenial qualities of the Third World client.

Most of all, social caseworkers and the social work profession seem to utilize the standards and values of white middle class America for determining the criteria of behavior that require acceptance and/or nonacceptance. The culture of the ethnic and racial group is usually ignored or placed in a subordinate position. Most workers, Black and non-Black alike, find it difficult to apply the principle of acceptance to behavior that differs from their own culture. This is more particularly the case when the worker may be aspiring to white middle class American values or when a worker is uncomfortable with the class or status in which he/she belongs. In the area of assessing middle class values and **acceptance**, the following case illustration between a Black worker and Black client will highlight potential difficulties that may occur:

> Mr. U., an unwed father, along with his girlfriend, Miss F., came to visit my office to discuss plans for the future. The unwed father did not have a job, and I was questioning him about his financial responsibility to the unborn baby. Miss F. had indicated that she did not have a job nor any money to pay for the birth of the baby. The unwed father informed me that he did not prefer a laboring job but he was an excellent gambler, poker player and pool shooter. He assured me that he could win enough money to support the birth of the coming infant.

> I explored with Mr. U. the uncertainty, inconsistency and insecurity of gambling as opposed to saving from a regular job. As the interview emerged, I provided support by agreeing to meet him on a weekly basis to look at his accomplishments as a pool player. It was agreed that if this approach was not successful, then we would consider other alternatives.

It is likely that the principle of acceptance would have been difficult to actualize by many workers because the values inherent in the American Protestant Work Ethic denote hard work, accountability and responsibility. Given the values of social work rooted in the Protestant Work Ethic, the worker may have been provoked to respond to the client by:

> Verbal persuasion on the virtues of economic stability associated with a steady job.

12

The morals of gambling as a way of life.

Verbal persuasion on the chance and risk involved in gambling.

Verbal persuasion on being responsible and accountable.

View of the client as resisting in the relationship.

In the worker/client situation described above, the uncongenial and negative feelings and attitude of the client regarding work may not be easy for a worker to accept. This is not to suggest that the worker should necessarily have had to approve of the client's behavior personally in order to demonstrate **acceptance**; but in order to be an effective worker, practitioners need to recognize that they work within the parameters of a culture. A client comes to an agency for help to modify or make adjustments within his/her environment or psychological make-up. Therefore, it is accepted that the worker is there to assist the client in making those adjustments. It is then the responsibility of the worker to accept the client without denoting or placing guilt or blame on the client's behavior but to work to assist the client in confronting and testing this adjustment to reality. Acceptance cannot be accomplished by merely accepting and reinforcing the positive disposition of the client and rejecting the negative disposition of the client's behavior.

In addition to the above, social caseworkers must do away with the "liberal" premise of "freedom from racial and ethnic prejudices." This premise mitigates the principle of **acceptance** in that the worker may be confronted with proving and justifying his/her liberalism to the point that it hampers an effective therapeutic relationship.

The notion of "proving acceptance" is not the proper use of the principle of **acceptance**. The

mere action of trying to prove **acceptance** or to
"prove" that one is not prejudice is a tacit indication of the opposite. The liberalism in
social work literature and the social work profession proposing such views as "the commonality
of human beings transcends racial and ethnic
differences"[8] and "identification with the
client's ego is to identify on a human level
which supersedes race and ethnicity,"[9] prohibit
genuine **acceptance.** Such liberal dispositions
prohibit the opportunity for the worker to develop self-awareness, self-insight and growth as
well as prohibit the opportunity for workers to
address the inherent negative myths and stereotypes that may interfere with looking at the
client "as he/she really is."

First and foremost, the social caseworker must be
comfortable with acceptance of self in relationship to Third World individuals as well as the
racial or ethnic group in which he/she belongs.
This is an area that presents much difficulty for
many social casework practitioners. For example,
in the presence of People of Color, the white
social caseworker may adopt the view that, "I
just happen to be white," "I just happen to be a
member of the majority race," or "I am human
first and white second," as an apology for the
atrocities that the white society may have perpetuated against such racial groups. In this instance, the white individual is saying that he/she
could have been "Black" or a member of any other
racial group, and he/she has provided an escape
for having any association with what the white
race may have done to People of Color. Most of
all, the white worker may be saying that he/she
sympathizes with the oppression of People of
Color and identify with the racial struggle in
spite of the fact that he/she is a member of the
white race.

On the other hand, there are Blacks and other
People of Color who cry, "I happen to be Mexican
or Black," "I am human first and Black second,"
or "I am a social worker first and Black second,"

14

as a means of de-emphasizing their racial/ethnic identity and identifying with the positive qualities attached to being "human" or a member of a profession. White is defined in the American culture as the epitomy of that which is human. Blacks are not white; therefore, they are considered nonhuman. In order to justify their existence as people of worth, many racial groups prefer to see themselves as being **human** rather than being People of Color.

First of all, it is not **accidental** that an individual is born into a particular ethnic group. Such action is predetermined without request or permission of the person involved. Yet, there appears to be an attempt on the part of many Third World caseworkers to assign uncongenial and negative myths to their own racial group by disassociating themselves from their racial grouping, saying "I happen to be Black." In order for a worker to be effective in a therapeutic relationship with a client of the same or different ethnic group, the worker must liberate self from all the negative assumptions and inferior qualities assigned to his/her ethnic identity. At the same time, the worker must proceed in destroying the negative myths and stereotypes associated with People of Color. Oftentimes, the negative assumptions and stereotypes associated with minority clients interfere with the process of **acceptance** between white worker and Black client and Black worker and Black client.

The above is not to suggest that a worker should acquiesce to his/her present social status in the society in order to facilitate **acceptance**. Instead, there must be a reinforcement of the notion that improvement in "role" and "status" in the society is not associated with "better" or "superior" in regard to race but viewed as being merely different. Class and culture are merely different from one another and not "superior" or "inferior" to one another.

Role of the Worker

The role of the social caseworker with People of Color in America as related to the principle of **acceptance** is as follows:

> Look at culture/ethnicity and race as being merely different and not superior or inferior to one another.
>
> Recognize, acknowledge and identify the cultural and ethnic biases and prejudices that may exist in self and are debilitating to the principles of **acceptance.**
>
> Recognize and accept the fact that "total freedom" from ethnic prejudices is impossible, but identify the area of conflict where worker is apt to coerce his/her views in making the client what "you want him to be."
>
> Assess, recognize and confront feelings of racism and elitism regarding members of different racial and ethnic groups.
>
> Develop self-awareness and self-insight in relation to race and culture.

NON-JUDGMENTAL ATTITUDE

According to the principle of **non-judgmental attitude**:

> Conviction that the casework function excludes assigning guilt or innocence, or degree of client's responsibility for causation of the problems or needs, but does include making evaluative judgments about the attitude, standards or action of the client. The attitude which involves both thought and feeling

elements is transmitted to the client.[10]

In the practice of social work, the assignments of "good" or "bad" and "guilt" or "innocence" to the behavior and attitudes of a client are contradictory to social work values. The development of prejudices and judgments is a natural part of the socialization process for individuals, however blatant or subtle. In the context of social casework with People of Color in America, the negative ingrained values within the American society regarding Black, Puerto Ricans and other minorities are so well socialized into individuals until it is impossible for **any** person to have escaped the effects. In any instance, the perpetuation of those socialization processes are sometimes so subtle that they may go unnoticed.

Subtle indications of the manifestation of stereotypes as they affect People of Color can be seen in many examples of the socialization process in America. It is the "good guys" who wear the **white** hats and the "bad guys" who wear the **black** hats. In an old television commercial there was a duel between a white knight and a black knight, and invariably the white knight won. In grocery stores of the American society one will find that there are white (angel's food) and black (devil's food) cakes. These factors, looked at in a vacuum or separately from the components of culture, may appear to be of little significance. Nonetheless, as we closely analyze the relationship between culture, language and white supremacy,[11] we will find that these examples are merely indicators and reflectors of the culture. The relevance of this thesis is applicable to all People of Color in America.

It is a challenge for minority and non-minority social casework practitioners alike to be **non-judgmental** when the society in which they live has denigrated People of Color with negative definitions and assumptions. If one would pick

up any dictionary, he/she will find "black" defined as:

> The word blackness has synonyms, 60
> of which are distinctly unfavorable,
> and none of them even mildly posi-
> tive. Among the offending 60 were
> such words as: blot, smut, smudge,
> sullied, begrime, soot, becloud, ob-
> scure, dingy, murky, low-tones,
> threatening, frowning, foreboding,
> forbidding, sinister, baneful, dis-
> mal, thundery, wicked, malignant,
> deadly, unclean, dirty, unwashed,
> foul, etc. In addition, 20 of those
> words, and I exclude the villianous
> 60 above, are related directly to
> race, such as "Negro," "Negress,"
> "nigger," "darkey," "blackamoor,"
> etc.[12]

By the same token, the concept white has a cor-
respondingly positive definition as found in Web-
ster. The positive definitions of white are as
detrimental to the social casework relationship
as the negative definitions of black. According
to the definition of white and whiteness:

> The word whiteness has 134 synonyms.
> 44 of which are favorable and pleas-
> ing to contemplate. For example:
> purity, cleanness, immaculate,
> bright, shiny, ivory, fair, blond,
> stainless, clean, clear, chase, un-
> blemished, unsullied, innocent, hon-
> orable, upright, just, straightfor-
> ward, fair, genuine, trustworthy...[13]

People of Color are made up of Black Americans,
Native Americans, Puerto Ricans, Mexican-Americans and others; and the definitions above have
implications for them all. For a more definitive
description and understanding of the relationship
between the definitions, language, culture, People of Color and non-judgmental attitudes, we
must understand the correlation between

these variables. First of all, there appears to be a causal relation whereby language influences culture, culture influences language and thought, and thought and culture influence language. Language is seen by many as a transmitter of culture, thereby substantiating the fact that the definitions of white and black are not in isolation or in a vacuum from the culture.[14] Therefore, the definition and description of People of Color in the American society cannot be viewed as separate components of the society, and prejudgments are implicit in the cultural definitions of the Third World minorities.

It is impossible for any caseworker, despite ethnicity and race, to be completely free from the contaminations of the negative judgments depicting minorities. Therefore, these negative variables interfere with the worker/client relationship between all clients and workers. The tasks faced by social caseworkers are to determine if their judgmental attitude is of such a nature that it may prohibit effective casework with clients. Secondly, the caseworkers must be cognizant of the judgmental attitudes he/she possesses and attempt to control those attitudes from manifesting themselves in the casework relationship. Because the feelings and attitudes of the worker are transmitted to the client, the social caseworker's willingness to expose and confront his/her insecurities and inadequacies regarding ethnicity and race in the casework relationship is a major step of progress for mitigating a **non-judgmental attitude**. It is impossible for a worker to be totally free of prejudices regarding race and ethnicity. Therefore, the possession of prejudices is permissible, but when a worker acts on these prejudices and stereotypes, it is destructive in the relationship. It is permissable for a worker to be selective about the ethnic or racial group with which he/she chooses to work just as caseworkers may choose to be selective about the social problem area they prefer to work. Traditionally, individual social workers have not been penalized

19

for their preferences in working with the handicapped, blind, aged and others. This practice is
crucial to the principle of **non-judgmental attitude** because the attitude (of the worker), which
involves both thought and feelings, is transmitted to the client. The following case illustration below will dramatize the complexity of sensitivity, perception, and prejudices involved in
the non-judgmental attitude process.

> Miss P., an unwed pregnant mother,
> visited my office during the early
> stages of her pregnancy to discuss plans
> for the baby. I raised a series of
> questions regarding the plans for the
> baby, as she appeared to be in a des-
> perate situation concerning her future.
> I asked such questions as "have you
> thought about giving the baby up for
> adoption," "have you thought about get-
> ting married," "have you thought about
> giving the baby to your mother to keep
> as you finish high school," and "have
> you thought about an abortion"?

The worker's supervisor called him in the office
the following morning and said jokingly, "I hear
that you are advocating abortions to clients."
In fact, the worker did not verbally advocate nor
suggest an abortion to the young unwed mother.
The question of abortion was among a series of
questions that the worker had raised with the
client. Yet, the client had perceived the questions on abortion to be filled with a moral
judgment. Did the worker transmit some thoughts
and feelings to the client?

In social casework with People of Color and the
implementation of **non-judgmental attitude**, the
worker is not to assume that his/her cultural
norm is such that the client must imitate the
worker in seeking a resolution to the problem
presented. Therefore, there is no room for the
assignment of guilt or innocence or good or bad
to the client's behavior. Such assignments and
actions on the part of the worker interfere with

the **non-judgmental attitude** principle and process in that the client will begin to devalue his/her innate strengths and self-worth. It is impossible for, a **non-judgmental attitude** to exist if the worker adopts a superior attitude that, "I have the answers to your problems," and "You must adopt my values if you are to conquer these difficulties." The above phenomenon is particularly prevalent in the cases where the minority worker and client are of the same ethnic and racial group.

Non-judgmental attitude is not in opposition to "making evaluative judgments about the attitudes, standards or actions of the client." However, these evaluative judgments must be used as reflective discussions in helping clients to reach the goals they are setting for themselves. Most important of all, these "evaluative judgments" must be reflective of the moral and ethical values of "right" and "wrong" in the client's culture.

Social casework practitioners must begin to look at social behavior as functional and dysfunctional rather than "good" or "bad" or "right" and "wrong." In other words, the behaviors of clients are purposeful and must be viewed in objective behavioral terms rather than value laden concepts like normal/abnormal, deviant/nondeviant, good/bad, righteous/evil, sinful/nonsinful. Such concepts as "good" and "bad" are heavily value laden with subjective judgments rather than focusing on the specific function of the client's behavior in objective terms. Each individual must be viewed as striving to obtain self-fulfillment and self-actualization, with some individuals having more of a capacity to achieve this status than others. It is the responsibility of the caseworker to make an evaluative judgment on the factors inherent in the client's life as well as the client's environment that may prohibit him/her from achieving the goals of self-actualization. This view of identifying behaviors, expressions, attitudes and actions in objective terminology will link the relationship between behavior and its cause. The notion of "good" and "bad" and "right" and "wrong" are attitudinal in nature, cannot be measured in behavioral terms and are reflective of subjective thought.

Role of the Worker

The role of the caseworker in actualizing the non-judgmental attitudes with People of Color should be kept in the following perspectives:

View behavior as functional and dys-functional with the role of the worker being to assist the client in modifying his/her environment or psychological status to obtain self-fulfillment and self-actualization.

Recognize that the movement toward non-judgmental attitude is deeply related to the acceptance of the premise that any negative feelings, however con-scious or unconscious, may be communi-cated to the client tacitly and overtly.

Attempt to establish early in the rela-tionship the feelings and attitudes about the client having a worker as a member of his/her race, ethnicity or a different race/ethnicity.

Adopt the view that all human beings are "treatable" in a therapeutic rela-tionship.

Recognize that differences in the Third World minority culture and the white majority culture are real issues but not the basis on which to determine be-havior.

CLIENT SELF-DETERMINATION

Client **self-determination** is an all encompassing principle that governs every aspect of the casework relationship. According to Biestek, client **self-determination** is:

> The practical recognition of the right and need of clients to freedom in making their own choices and decisions in the casework process. Caseworkers have a corresponding duty to respect that right, recognize that need, stimulate and help to activate that potential for self-direction by helping the client to see and use the available and appropriate resources of the community and of his own personality. The client's right to self-determination, however, is limited by the client's capacity for positive and constructive decision-making by the framework of civil and moral law and by the function of the agency.[15]

In the principle of **self-determination,** the worker must recognize and accept the unequivocal right of the human being to make decisions for self and accept the consequences of those decisions.

Secondly, the worker must recognize the basic right of a human being to fail, if he/she so chooses, without the intervention of forces by the worker to prevent him/her from failure. As stated in the definition of **self-determination,** the only limitation placed on the right of self-determination is when the client's right interferes with moral and civil law. The failure of a client to succeed must be viewed as a non-negotiable right. Failure may be viewed as a "stepping stone to success."

Social caseworkers must abolish the attitude of "joy in victory" and "agony in defeat" when working with clients. This is not a win or lose situation, and the results in therapy, whether positive or negative, "are not about the therapist." The purposefulness of behavior necessitates that workers should look at all actions and behaviors on the part of the client as a "learning experience" for the client. As far as the worker is concerned, the old medical adage that, "You can have a successful operation but the patient dies," applies. On the other hand, the above assumptions do not rule out genuine empathy, concern and sincerity toward the client. Simultaneously, there is no "wrong" or "right" decision on the part of an individual client in determining his/her future. All decisions are made on the basis of options and possible consequences and the client's knowledge of what those consequences might be. A client is never aware of all the options nor does he/she have control over all of them. Yet, there are specific difficulties pertaining to the social casework practice and **self-determination** of Third World minority clients. Some of them are as follows:

Caseworker's view of the client's failures as reflection of the worker's effectiveness and ability to relate to People of Color.

Subtle view of the profession that a worker's lack of success with People of Color in America as an indication of insecurities, inadequacies and adjustment problems of the worker.

Glorified professional praise for both minority and majority worker on demonstration of an effectiveness with clients of different racial and ethnic groups.

The prevailing assumption in the American society of Third World people as incapable of making effective decisions regarding their lives.

Self-determination is easily realized by the social casework practitioner who trusts humanity to think and make choices for themselves, that is, people learn best by their own trials and errors to resolve problems. Wisdom is gained through experience and is not transferred through advice. In working with People of Color the practitioner will not foster **self-determination** when the knowledge of human behavior from a cultural perspective is either overlooked or misunderstood. It is the responsibility of the worker in the process of stimulating **self-determination** to utilize the systematic approach of deductive reasoning and reflective discussions to assist the client in reaching his/her decision. It is the client who must ultimately implement the goals of therapy. There are many untold stories involving clients who have attempted to follow the advice of practitioners, but failed. Therefore, the role of the social caseworker with People of Color may be as follows in regard to self-determination.

Recognize and accept the fact that self-determination is a God-given right and self-determination must be viewed from a cultural context.

An example of **self-determination** being implemented from a cultural dimension can be seen in the case illustration of **Mrs. D.,** a Puerto Rican mother. According to the social caseworker:

> Mrs. D.'s mother used to pay for her grandson's boarding school tuition through the rental of part of her large house in Puerto Rico. Following the grandmother's death, Mrs. D. flew back to New York City from Puerto Rico, leaving all financial details to be worked out by her uncle because she was too grieved over the death of her mother to attend to those matters.

Lacking the house rental income, she
was forced to remove her son from the
school where he had been doing well.
She went to a therapist when her son
began to act out after living in a slum
area for the first time. The therapist
discovered that it was the first time
the child had acted out and the behavior was related to the boy's removal
from the school where he had been
happy. The therapist explored
Mrs. D.'s fantasy and discovered that
she had expected her uncle to continue
to rent part of the house without her
having to ask him; she was very good to
him and placed herself in his hands.
The therapist encouraged Mrs. D. to go
to Puerto Rico and confront her uncle
with the fact that as the only daughter, the house belonged to her.[16]

The intricacies of family life, kinship, roles
and relationships in the Puerto Rican family prohibited the client from engaging in an open confrontation with her uncle to resolve the problem;
yet, this would have been the middle class
"American way." In the eyes of a social caseworker who may not be familiar with Puerto Rican
culture, it may have appeared appropriate for a
confrontation to occur between the client and her
uncle in order for the monies to be obtained.
The unaware caseworker may have been working to
help the client overcome her fears of overt confrontation with uncle and the psychological
factors underlying those fears.

Caseworkers must recognize where their right to
self-determination begins and ends and where the
self-determination of the client's begins and
ends. They must also be cognizant of the specific cultural life-stypes of Third World minorities and utilize the unique cultural variables to
implement solutions to the presenting problem.

In many cases, it may be difficult for a social

caseworker to utilize the cultural dimensions and variables of a particuar minority group culture in fostering self-determination because the values of social work may be antithetical to the very foundation of the Third World minority's culture. Consequently, such actions may appear to undermine the essence of social work knowledge and threaten the "authority" and vested interest of the social work profession. A case illustration describing the principle of noninterference in Native American culture will explain the dynamics further:

> The following incident illustrates noninterference in the simplest of matters. I was visiting my cousins when one of them put on his coat and said he was going downtown. He had no car, so one could assume he was going to walk. I restated his intention and volunteered to drive him. The cousin showed noninterference with my activities by not asking or even suggesting that I drive him, although that is certainly what he wanted. If he had asked directly and I had not cared to drive him, I would have been put on the spot. I would have been forced to refuse unobligingly or agree unwillingly. But by simply putting on his coat and announcing his intentions, he allowed me to accept or reject his desires without causing bad feelings for anyone. I could volunteer to take him or pay no attention to his actions.

> A cross-cultural misunderstanding might occur in the following way: A non-Indian guest at my mother's home, having enjoyed a rice dinner, might pay this compliment: 'Your rice was so good! I should be happy to have your recipe, if I may. And do you want some of my rice recipes in exchange?' The offered recipes might strengthen

friendship among Anglos, but to an
Indian it cancels the compliment. If
my mother had wanted other recipes, she
would have suggested it to her guest.
When the guest makes the offer on her
own initiative, it implies she did not
really care for my mother's rice and
knows a better way to prepare it. If
the guest had talked only about various
ways of preparing rice, she would have
given my mother the opportunity to ask
about any that interested her.[17]

In addition to dramatizing the inconsistency in
applied social casework techniques to resolve the
problem, the above is a paramount illustration of
the use of the cultural variable in social work
intervention to foster **self-determination**. The
notion of noninterference implicit in the
American Indian culture prohibits the traditional
approaches of casework practice and the fostering
of **self-determination**. Some of the roles of the
social caseworker practitioner and **self-
determination** with People of Color include the
following:

Must have a genuine internalized belief and trust in the rights of individual freedom.

Must empathize with the experiences
of Third World clients through an understanding of their culture as solutions are sought to the problems.

Must do away with the need to "stan-
dardize" and generalize options in
behavior as being acceptable only if
they fall within norms of the majority culture.

Must not view the freedom of choices
and options chosen by a client's behavior as a rejection of the practitioner.

Must recognize that the foundation and epitomy of effective casework practice is to assist the client in reaching decisions based on alternatives rather than providing advice from the worker's perspective and cultural view.

PURPOSEFUL EXPRESSION OF FEELINGS

According to Biestek, **purposeful expression of feeling is:**

The recognition of the client's need to express his feelings, especially his negative feelings. The caseworker listens purposefully, neither discouraging nor condemning the expression of these feelings, sometimes even actively stimulating them when they are therapeutically useful as part of the casework service.[18]

The major ingredients of **purposeful expression of feelings** are (1) freedom of expression, (2) expression of negative feelings, (3) purposeful listening of the worker, (4) neither condemning nor discouraging negative feelings and (5) actively stimulating negative feelings when they are therapeutically useful. In social casework with People of Color, the worker must particularly stimulate and encourage negative expressions and feelings without condemnation or discouragement as it may pertain to the client's view of the worker. Therefore, a key and significant aspect of **purposeful expression of feelings** in regard to social casework with People of Color is the encouragement of those negative feelings as they are **directed toward the worker's race and ethnicity.** It may be easy for the caseworker to encourage negative feelings as long as those feelings are directed away from the worker. The degree of emotional anxiety, insecurity and self-exposure is heightened on the part of the worker when those negative feelings are directed toward him/her. The dynamics are the same even in the relationship between minority worker and client of the same or different minority groups.

The nature and dynamics of the relationships among workers and clients of different racial and ethnic groups make the question of the client's race an important variable. The question of racial differences should be raised early in the relationship. This is not to suggest that all problems of a particular client may relate to specific concerns of race or ethnicity. However, in cases where there are racial concerns, the worker will never be able to get to the more subtle problems that a client may bring to the relationship until the racial and ethnic concerns are addressed. The rationale for addressing the question of race, for the worker, is to build a bridge for candid and honest dialogue in the be- ginning that may prevent other problems as the case progresses. It is much easier for the worker to address this concern early in the rela- tionship than to attempt to address the issue once the relationship becomes solidified.

Another aspect of social casework with People of Color related to **purposeful expression of feelings** is the inability of the worker to inter- pret the cultural experiences of Third World clients and reply or listen purposively. Often- times, the life experiences of individuals from the Third World differ so much from that of majority workers until the worker is rendered in- effective. For example, the experiences of witchcraft and voodoo as part of the Third World minority cultural experiences may extend beyond the constellation of non-minority cultures and social caseworkers may find it difficult to pene- trate the cultural life of such a client. The case of **Mr. M.** will provide another perspective to **purposeful expression of feelings** with a Third World minority client.

Mr. M. was a 40 year-old Spanish American. When he was 35, his somewhat dominating mother had died, and he had moved, with his wife and six children, to Denver. He soon discovered that his wife could obtain work more easily than he. He began to miss his home and to resent his wife's increasing independence. When he was 40, he began to think his wife was having an affair with one of his friends. He beat her up, and she obtained an order for hospitalization on three occasions, and in the process, she obtained a legal separation. As his illness progressed he also became more obviously depressed. His last admission, when I began to treat him, was precipitated by his hearing voices urging him to kill himself.

He has always arrived at the hospital mute and agitated. Though he would eventually respond to medication, he would never talk about his problem, and upon discharge he would stop his medication and refuse follow-up care. Once, however, he joined the other Spanish-America patients to complain that a Spanish patient had been secluded because of Anglo prejudice.

Initially all he would say to me was, 'I just want to be a normal American.' I acknowledged his right to desire this but asked if he felt this had been denied him. He eventually expressed considerable hostility toward Anglos. After this, he began to express his anger at his wife for 'bossing' him around, vowed to divorce her, and seemed very well. Following his discharge, he took his medication and came to see me regularly.

One day he cautiously revealed that he had also been seeing a **curandera** (female folk healer) for 'stomach troubles.' She had sworn him to secrecy, but he promised to tell me more at the next session.

The next time he seemed upset and reported having had persecutory dreams. Eventually, he said that the **curandera** had not merely given him an olive tonic but had also expressed an interest in his life and had commented that he seemed lonely. He thought she was offering to be his mistress, became frightened, and said he would never see her again. Instead, he returned to his wife. This went well until she refused to have intercourse. I wondered if his return to his wife was wise. I never saw him again. Three months later his wife called to inquire about the bill. She incidentally mentioned that he had killed himself. She had found my telephone number in his pocket.[19]

One may suggest that the inability of the worker to **purposefully** listen to and interpret the client's experience and cultural orientation is what eventually led the client to a "folk healer." It is difficult to infer that the inability of the worker to intervene vicariously into the cultural life of the client is what led to the client's death. However, the social caseworker practitioners must realize the necessity to vicariously enter the client's cultural experience while maintaining enough objectivity to assist the client in the resolution of his/her problem.

Secondly, the worker must recognize the value of **purposeful** listening as well as **purposeful expressions of feelings** as it may pertain to the psychological understanding of the client's cultural world view. It is accepted that **purposeful**

32

expressions of feelings includes the "recognition of the client's need to express self freely and the caseworker listens purposefully without discouraging nor condemning those feelings." However, little mention is made of the worker's role in working with People of Color by stimulating the work environment to facilitate the therapeutic relationship. This is not to suggest that the worker should engage in artificial and superficial arrangements of his/her office or to change his/her dress decor as a means of encouraging purposeful expression or identification with the client's culture. Nonetheless, the genuine appreciation of the ethnic/racial cultural values should demonstrate itself in the physical as well as the social arrangements of the facilities in the office. The case illustration below will dramatize the dynamics further:

> After a few months of individual contact with Abdulla, an eleven-year-old youth diagnosed as a juvenile delinquent, I noticed that when in my office he would sit on the edge of his seat and resist dialogue in the interview process. On one occasion my office was being used by another social worker and we had to use the conference room. He appeared more relaxed and ready for dialogue during this interview.

> Periodically, Abdulla and I would go to the recreational hall to play pool or basketball. I noticed that the client was completely free in expressing himself when playing games or in the conference room.

> As I analyzed the office arrangements, I noted that the eleven-year-old youth was seated directly in front of me as I sat behind the desk. In the conference room, the seating was arranged in a circle, and while we played games there were no seating arrangements at all.

Therefore, it dawned on me that the seating arrangements, with me behind the desk and the client on the other side of the desk, was the imitation of authority and victim as presented in the school situation where he had difficulty with authority.

In relation to People of Color who are institutionalized, there are other significant factors that must be considered in regard to **purposeful expression of feelings.** In social agencies, hospitals, juvenile centers and prisons, it is necessary for the music and programming on the radio and television to reflect the minority culture. There are patients in mental hospitals who are unable to appear well groomed because the hospitals do not provide Afro hair combs in order for the patients to comb their hair. The combs that are available will not penetrate the hair of an African-American. These factors of purposeful expression of feelings are not considered in Biestek's model, but are very crucial to an effective therapeutic relationship between institution, worker and Third World minority clients. It is accepted by members of the Caucasian race that they will hear music and have available reading material to relate to their cultural orientation when they enter a doctor's office or clinic, and this added stimulation provides a source of relief. However, many minority clients approach a doctor's office or clinic with suspiciousness based on being a minority member and are provided no visual or auditory stimulations for relaxation. The development of an effective therapeutic relationship with Third World minority clients may be aided by providing an environment that relates to the client's cultural orientation.

It is the responsibility of social caseworker practitioners to be innovative and experiental in determining how they may demonstrate authentic interpersonal professional relationships through purposeful expressions of feelings.

Role of the Caseworker

Some of the roles for caseworker in implementing **purposeful expressions of feelings** may be the following:

> Cognitive knowledge about the human and phychological growth/development of individuals from Third World cultures.
>
> Assumption that People of Color can accept the genuine and authentic feelings and behaviors of social caseworkers.
>
> Authentic acceptance and appreciation of Third World minority cultures coupled with the arrangements of the therapeutic environment to facilitate effective casework process.
>
> Vicariously penetrating the thought and culture processes of the unique experiences of Third World minority clients.
>
> Stimulation and encouragement of the negative expressions of feelings experienced by the client, particularly those directed toward the worker.

CONTROLLED EMOTIONAL INVOLVEMENT

Another principle of the casework relationship as composed by Biestek is **controlled emotional involvement,** which is defined as:

> The caseworker's sensitivity to the client's feelings, and understanding of their meaning and a purposeful appropriate response to the client's feelings.[20]

In working with People of Color and utilizing the principles of **controlled emotional involvement,** the basic negative assumptions that must be eradicated are:

Helping a minority client is helping the "cause" of minority people.

In working with Third World minority clients both majority and minority workers must first do away with the notion that engaging in a casework relationship with Third World minority clients is somehow associated with uplifting the plight and cause of the entire minority race or ethnic group. The minority client is an **individual** who comes to the worker with an **individual** problem even though the problem presented may have implications and overtones related to oppression from being a member of a minority group. It must be remembered that this is an individual client with an individual problem.

Too often, Third World minority clients are symbolic of the entire race or ethnic group with which the client is associated.

The assumption of the worker that he/she is helping the "entire race/ethnic group" prohibits the foundation of **controlled emotional involvement**. In traditional social casework, **controlled emotional involvement** was interpreted by many to mean an emotional detachment and aloofness from the client and his/her problem. This new phenomenon is not to be associated with aloofness and detachment. Social casework with minority clients should be highly involved, with no limitations or restrictions on emotional sensitivity and feedback. The response of the worker to the client must be appropriate and not contaminated with the worker's need to "do for client."

Controlled emotional involvement implies an objective "restraint" and "withholding," but inherent in this definition of control is an active and appropriate response. This respose is important in social casework with People of Color because of the following prevailing negative assumption.

Third World minority clients cannot accept the authentic feelings and behaviors of majority and minority workers.

The issue of authentic relations is of particular importance when there is a relationship between worker and client of different racial groups. The worker may have difficulty in addressing certain aspects of the therapeutic relationship for fear that the client cannot accept the authentic observation and interpretation of the worker. This assumption presents a posture of superiority on the part of the worker and is damaging to the concept of **controlled emotional involvement** and the therapeutic relationship.

Controlled emotional involvement implies that the worker will be authentic and purposeful in utilizing self and all available techniques of social casework to help the client confront self and the problems faced in finding a solution to the difficulties. As the practice of social casework with minorities emerges, social casework practitioners may use any aspect of a client's cultural background as a springboard for the therapeutic process. Therefore, the use of the horoscope, Holy Bible, the Koran and other facets of the individual's life and culture may be engaged as a basis for entering into the psychic function of the client. This is not to suggest that the worker is to have a particular belief in those philosophies, but that they may become mere tools for stimulating communication needed to assist in providing a solution to the individual problem of the client.

The emotional closeness that often develop between worker and client of different ethnic groups provides a natural inclination on the part of the worker to explore the "unknown" in order to fulfill the personal fantasies hidden deep in his/her unconsciousness. The most frequently aroused fantasy between worker and client of different ethnic groups is related to sexual stereotypes. These fantasies may be provoked by the client and/or stimulated by the worker. If the worker concludes from his/her observations that there is a sexual attraction on the part of the client or if there is a mutual attraction, controlled emotional involvement should apply. The worker must provide an appropriate response and sensitivity to the client's feelings, and the dynamics must be understood in relationship to the client's problem. In the Black/white worker/client relationship this is a complex matter. If there is a sexual attraction on the part of the worker to the client, the worker must recognize the handicaps involved. The worker must have an appropriate appraisal of his/her own subjective feelings. In either case, appropriate responses in **controlled emotional involvement** may be as follows:

Acknowledge the sexual attraction to self (worker); verbally acknowledge the sexual attraction to client.

Verbally acknowledge the sexual attraction (worker response to client).

Discuss therapeutic relevance of the sexual attraction (worker and client).

The most detrimental dynamics possible in a situation of sexual attraction between worker and client is for the worker to ignore the client's sexual attraction or for the worker to deny that he/she is sexually attracted to the client. As stated in the principal of **non-judgmental attitude**, the denied feelings and emotions in a relationship will have more of a profound effect on the casework relationship than the manifested dialogue. In cases where there is an unconscious conspiracy between worker and client to avoid discussion of certain factors, the damage is more severe in that the unconscious denied factors interfere with the conscious material discussed. Above all, there is more of an opportunity for fluid movement in a case once the unconscious avoided material is ventilated. The following

38

case illustration between a Black worker and Black client dramatizes the factors discussesd:

> Miss J., a twenty-three-year old Black female and the mother of two young children, was coming to see me so that I could assist her with her feelings following a recent divorce. It was my primary assignment to assist Miss J. in working with the welfare department for materials and helping her to acquire an apartment of her own. I was in graduate school and this was my first field placement.
>
> As our contacts continued, I noticed that the client was becoming an impeccable dresser and she would leave her children with neighbors or relatives. She would sit in front of my desk with her short dresses showing her upper thigh. I was being sexually attracted to the client but did not want to recognize it.
>
> I never told my supervisor about this ambivalent sexual attraction I had for the client, and I never discussed this matter with the client. However, I found myself doing things for the client in helping her get materials from the welfare department, which the client should have been doing for herself. In fact, I found myself unconsciously conspiring with the client to assist her in defrauding the welfare department.
>
> During one of my supervisory sessions, my supervisor pointed to material in my case recordings and wondered if I were sexually attracted to the client. I was able to acknowledge and accept my attractions for Miss J. and introduce this material in therapy. Following

the discussion of our mutual sexual attraction, the temptation ceased and
therapy progressed.

Role of the Worker

In order for effective **controlled emotional involvement** to take place with People of Color, the
following factors must be considered:

The workers must feel free to take
risks in exposing his/her perceptions
of the client's feelings and behaviors
in the therapeutic process.

The worker must not interpret **controlled emotional involvement** as an
"aloofness" and "detachment," but rather a rigorous and highly involved
experience.

Sensitivity to feelings and **controlled
emotional involvement** include exposi-
tion of overt feelings as well as the
more hidden feelings and behavior of a
client in the therapeutic process.

The worker must recognize that "I may
be part of the problem."

Helping a Third World minority client
is not helping the entire race and ethnic group.

Over-identification with client due to
race or ethnicity is detrimental to the
therapeutic process.

Control in emotional involvement merely
suggests that the action in the therapeutic process is accomplished by
assisting the client to function inde-
pendently in the environment and by
recognizing that the authentic behavior

of the worker is an important variable.

CONFIDENTIALITY

Biestek defines **confidentiality** as:

> The preservation of secret information
> concerning the client which is dis-
> closed in the professional relation-
> ship. Confidentiality is based upon a
> basic right of the client; it is an
> ethical obligation of the caseworker
> and is necessary for effective casework
> services. The client's right, however,
> is not absolute. Moreover, the
> client's secret is often shared with
> other professional persons within the
> agency and in other agencies...the ob-
> ligation then binds all.[21]

Confidentiality is one of those all-encompassing
principles in the casework relationship in that
it underlies each and every principle stipulated.
The systematic and historical violation of confidential material from People of Color by social
caseworkers from all races has made People of
Color most suspicious and reluctant to reveal material of a confidential nature.

Traditionally, **confidentiality** has been abused
and misused in the Third World community by the
majority race manipulating information out of
Third World minority members under the pretense
that such information would benefit the minorities, when in fact, the information was used for
the destruction of the minority interest. As far
as inter- and intra- minority relations and **confidentiality** are concerned, it has been a common
practice for a minority member to gather confidential information that would be used destruc-
tively toward the minority community.

It is important, then, to look at **confidentiality**
with People of Color as being more than a

"preservation of secret information," although this variable is important. The attitudinal dimension of **trust** and **confidence** must be intertwined with **confidentiality.** Otherwise, the client's trust and confidence in the caseworker's "preservation of secret information" is futile. The successful internalization and implementation of the principles of **individualization, acceptance, purposeful expressions of feelings, nonjudgmental attitude, controlled emotional involvement** and **self-determination** are the stimuli for the development of trust and confidence that will lead to the dynamic relation for gathering confidential information for therapeutic use.

Implicit in the principle of **confidentiality** is the element of the worker's respect for the individuality and personal well-being of the client as well as respect for the information given. It is essential that the worker engage in discussions early in the stages of the relationship with the client about the purpose, goals and parameters of **confidentiality.** Secondly, the attitude of confidentiality rests with the comfort and security of the worker in asking pertinent questions of the Third World minority client. For many reasons non-minority workers may feel hesitant to ask or uncover certain materials because the data may be different from the experiences they may know. This hesitancy may be transmitted to the client and misinterpreted to denote incompetence in the worker's skills.

Finally, the over-eagerness on the worker's part to gain information from the client may interfere with obtaining confidential information from a Third World minority client. For many social workers the first opportunity to experience an intensive relationship with someone of another ethnic group is in the worker/client relationship. Therefore, the eagerness to penetrate for information may handicap communication. Once this is detected by the client, confidentiality and trust are questioned in the relationship and rapport is endangered.

42

Role of the Worker

The behavioral manifestation of **confidentiality** is relatively easy to perform by the worker, but the attitudinal aspect of **confidentiality** and trust is more difficult. Therefore, the role of the worker in **confidentiality** may be as follows:

Preserve confidentiality (information).

Discuss and explain confidentiality early in the casework relationship.

Respect individual dignity and personal worth of Third World individuals.

Be aware of Third World minorities sensitivity to issues of confidentiality.

Believe in the intrinsic and non-negotiable right of confidentiality.

Recognize that breach of confidentiality is usually irreparable in a therapeutic relationship.

Enhance trust, confidence and communication using confidentiality as the medium.

Conclusion

The seven principles of the casework relationship must be viewed as part of a whole rather than as separate components. It is the negative assumptions about race and ethnicity that impede the use of the casework principles. The important role of negative and positive assumptions in the worker/client relationship cannot be overemphasized in regard to People of Color. It is natural for humans to operate out of certain assumptions regarding actions they may take. Sometimes, those assumptions are conscious; while other times, the assumptions may be unconscious.

It is necessary, then, for the worker to make and internalize positive assumptions rather than negative ones.

In conclusion, it is the responsibility of schools of social work and social work agencies to encourage caseworkers to make **positive** assumptions rather than negative assumptions that are destructive to the effective implementation of the principles of the casework relationship. Listed below are a few of the positive assumptions that social caseworker practitioners should internalize in their work with People of Color.

"I may be part of the problem."

People of Color have a heritage and culture of which they can be proud.

Be the first to confront the differences and conflicts in the worker/-client relationship.

Third World minority individuals desire to be independent and self-sufficient.

Expression of pro-ingroup ethnic and racial consciousness/pride is not necessarily anti-white.

Race/ethnicity is an important variable in the worker/client relationship.

People of Color can handle the authentic feelings and behavior of workers from other ethnic/racial groups.

1. Ignacio Aguilar. "Initial contacts with
    Mexican Americans," Social Work, (May 1972),
    p. 66.

2. Lois Pettit. "Some Observations on Negro
    Culture in the United States," Social Work
    Vol. 5, No. 3, (July 1960), p. 105.

3. David R. Burgest. "Racism in Everyday
    Language and Social Work Jargon," Social
    Work, Vol. 18, No. 4, (July 1973), pp. 22-25.

4. Felix Biestek. Casework Relationship
    London: University Books, (1967), p. 25

5. Esther Fibush. "The White Worker and the
    Negro Client," Social Casework, Vol. XVI,
    (May 1965), p. 274.

6. Felix Biestek. Casework Relationship,
    p. 72.

7. Harry L. Kitano and Roger Daniels. American
    Racism: Exploration of the Nature of
    Prejudice. Englewood Cliffs: Prentice-Hall,
    Inc., (1970), pp. 2-23.

8. Leonard C. Simmons. "'Crow Jim':
    Implications for Social Work," Social Work,
    Vol. 8, No. 3, (July 1963), p. 29.

9. Ibid, p. 26.

10. Felix Biestek. The Casework Relationship,
    p. 90.

11. David R. Burgest. "Racist Use of the
    English Language," The Black Scholar,
    (September 1973), p. 38.

12. Ossie Davis, "The English Language is My
    Enemy," in Arthur C. Smith, Language,
    Communication and Rhetoric in Black American,
    New York: Harper & Row, (1972), p. 74.

13. Ibid. p. 74.

14. Lloyd Yabura. "Toward a Language of
       Humanism: A Tool for Black Liberation,"
       Rhythm Magazine, (Summer 1971), p. 15.

15. Felix Biestek. The Casework Relationship,
       p. 103.

16. Sonia Badillo Ghali, "Culture, Sensitivity
       and the Puerto Rican Client," Social Work,
       (September 1975), p. 462.

17. Ronald G. Lewis and Man Keung Ho. "Social
       Work with Native Americans," Social Work,
       (September 1975), p. 381.

18. Felix Biestek. The Casework Relationship,
       p. 35.

19. Lawrence Y. Kline, "Some Factors in the
       Psychiatric Treatment of Spanish-Speaking
       Americans," American Journal of Psychiatry,
       Vol. 125, (1969), pp. 91-92.

20. Felix Biestek. The Casework Relationship,
       p. 50.

21. Ibid. p. 121.

Chapter II

PSYCHODYNAMICS OF SOCIAL CASEWORK
WITH
PEOPLE OF COLOR

Introduction:

This chapter will review, explore and analyze the progression of the historical relationship between the casework profession and People of Color. This historical relationship began with the interaction between the white worker and Black client and progresses to the contemporary interaction among other People of Color. A synthesis of the theoretical analyses and interpretations existing between scholars and practitioners on the worker/client relationship with People of Color will be provided. Secondly, the theoretical concepts and constructs underlying the foundation of social casework practice will be analyzed and evaluated for their relevance and applicability to Third World minority clients. Finally, there will be an exploration and evaluation of the unique culture and philosophical world view of ethnic European cultures. This analysis and exploration will provide the framework for building and developing a more solid theoretical base for the future.

WORLD VIEW/CULTURAL DIMENSION
OF
THIRD WORLD MINORITIES IN AMERICA

In the course of human history, men
have created numerous images of good
and evil; these in turn have served as
justification for forming cohesive
groups...that is, for including some
persons in the group and for excluding
others from it. In America, the two
most powerful such justifications relate to skin color (or race) and....[22]

The division of humankind along color lines is
reinforced by the philosophical epistemological
world view of People of Color and the epistemological world view of Caucasions. The epistemological world view of a people has a reciprocal
relationship with culture if, in fact, it is not
a determinant of culture. The relationship between world view and culture is similar in
character to the relationship between language
and culture in that some authorities see a reciprocal relationship between language and culture while others would have culture determine
the language. One resource puts it this way:

> 'World view' is an elusive term, but
> when we speak of someone's world view
> in any of its senses, we do not mean
> simply the world impressing itself upon
> his passive receptors, sensory or in-
> tellectual. A person does not receive
> a world view but rather takes or adopts
> one. A world view is not a datum, a
> danne, but something the individual
> himself of the culture he shares partly
> constructs.[23]

Epistemology refers to the origin of thought and
knowledge as it developed and emerged untold
generations ago and gives shape to how people
think, feel, behave and view their environment
from then until the present. World view denotes

the unique characteristics and dynamics manifested throughout the culture. Culture denotes the customs, traditions, way of life and beliefs of a people as dramatized in their social, political, religious and economical arrangements. Culture may be looked at in the following manner:

> Culture is that complex whole which includes knowledge, belief, act, morals, law, customs and any other capabilities and habits acquired by man as a member of society.[24]

Another source states that:

> The sum total of ways of living built up by a group of human beings and transmitted by one generation to another.[25]

Yet, another significant ingredient to the definition of culture refers to the conscious/unconscious dimension.

> Any shape or cluster of human history still apparent in the conscious/unconscious habit or groups of people is what is meant by culture.[26]

The relationship between world view and culture and its impact on individual behavior may best be dramatized through the following illustration:

> The client's aspirations for himself is likely to be in terms of the norms of his own culture unless he is trying to identify himself with a group other than of his family of orientation.[27]

The most profound impact of culture on individual behavior can be viewed from the perspective that:

> The individual finds opportunity to express his instinctual drives primarily within the social and cultural institu-

tions. His perception of the object world, organization of these perceptions into a meaningful whole, and judgment in choosing goals (all functions of the ego) are strongly influenced by the values of his culture and class.[28]

In spite of the fact that the ingredients of a culture are often spoken of as an absolute entity, culture must be viewed also as in a state of constant change. Therefore, the study of culture in relationship to individual functioning and perceptions must be continuously re-evaluated. One authority states:

Culture...for any group of people, is a dynamic process and is in a state of constant change. Caution must be taken not to create a cultural stereotype to which all members of a particular race/ethnicity group are expected to conform.[29]

Ultimately, it is difficult to say that the epistemological world view determines culture, but we know that what people thought and believed untold generations ago has a definite impact upon the shaping of society and culture as we know it today. Historians and social scientists are partly able to determine world view by analyzing and interpreting the mythologies of Western and Eastern people through the thinking of the Early Greek philosophers who originated the Western world view and African philosophers who originated the Eastern world view. People of Color are composed of the Negroid and Mongoloid races and make up the Eastern world view, and the Western world view is made up of the non-colored people of the world, commonly referred to as Caucasion.

WESTERN WORLD VIEW AND CULTURE

The unique ingredients and characteristics that make

up the European (Greek) epistemological conception of the universe and their relationship to other humans, God, and nature can best be illustrated by looking at their view of matter and entities in the universe. A close observation of the Western world view will reveal a separation of all forces, physical and nonphysical, into divisions and dichotomies. These forces, which are divided into oppositions and categories, are perceived to be at odds, in conflict with each other. This is demonstrated through the Western world view division and conflict between humans/-nature, God/Devil, cause/effect, organic/inorganic, mind/body, good/evil, and black/white, plus many others. The division and conflict inherent in Western world view can best be visualized as linear. It is speculated that the origin of divisions in Greek society has its beginning in their separating humans from nature. According to Cedric Clark:

> The Greek political state was a slave state. Even the most noble of the Greek thinkers, Aristotle, saw fit to justify the existence of slaves in Greek society...in separating themselves from other men, the Greeks, of necessity, separated themselves from nature as well as from man...for man was...even in the Early Greek legends considered to be an integral part of nature. One could not divorce himself from other men and still maintain a personal involvement with nature. But such a divorce did take place in the minds of the influential Greek thinkers and such a division is the cornerstone of contemporary Western (societies) scientific thinkers.[30]

Another key aspect to the existence of this conflict is seen in the negative, unfavorable definition of the concept black (blackness) and the positive, favorable definition of the concept white (whiteness). These negative definitions of blackness and positive definitions of whiteness were concomitantly transferred to Black people and white people. As one author puts it:

> Long before they found that men were Black, Englishmen found in the idea of blackness a way of expressing some of their most ingrained values. No color except white conveyed so much emotional impact.[31]

The generally-held assumption is that the origin of the notion of white supremacy began with the enslavement of Blacks and other colored people of the world (Indians) for economic expediency.[32] Many scholars of history and anthropology tell their students that the negativism of blackness and positiveness of whiteness were generated following the Europeans' observation of the African culture, which was uniquely different from their own. As history reveals, the European world view based in opposition and dichotomy between Black/white and humans/nature is responsible for the notion of supremacy of whiteness and inferiority of blackness. The fact that a negative definition of Black and positive definition of white existed long before Europeans were aware of Black people reinforces the premise that it was the epistemological world view of the Europeans that was responsible for the definitions. According to John O. Killens:

> All nonwhites throughout the world become 'niggers' and therefore, proper material for 'civilizing' and 'Christianizing' (cruel euphemism for colonization, exploitation, genocide, and slavery).[33]

EASTERN WORLD VIEW AND CULTURE

The epistemological world view of Eastern people is quite different from the Western world view. In traditional Eastern societies, people main-

maintained a belief in the essential unity of all things material and immaterial and fostered the maintenance of a harmonious relationship with God, humans, nature and the universe. There was no separation among matter, materials, forces and entities within the universe. There was no view of conflict between good/evil, humans/nature, cause/effect, mind/body and others in Eastern culture. In fact, the Eastern societies saw harmony and unity among all forces and entities in the culture and society. This concept of oneness, unity, cohesion and harmony is best visualized in the form of a circle.

In the words of Charles Frye:

> The most ancient symbol known to man is the black circle or disc. This symbol represents the source of all life, knowledge, understanding and truth. The black circle is the womb, the Great Mother, the container of all that has ever been, is now and ever will be. The black circle symbolizes the undifferentiated state of spirit and matter, light and darkness, good and evil, male and female and all other so-called opposites.[34]

In the same way that the early Greek philosophers built the foundation for Western thought, early African philosophers shaped the foundation for Eastern thought. According to one source:

> On the continent of Africa, scholars very much retained their belief in the essential unity of the most highly developed of the African sciences (i.e., Alchemy) insisted that spiritual forces (e.g., Incantation) were just as much a part of reality as were the chemicals with which they were working. In the Northern part of Africa, man saw his observation of the hemisphere tied up with forests and rivers. In both

cases, as well as in many parts of the
Eastern and Southern American world,
man did not see himself separated from
nature and significantly from other
men.[35]

The impact of the Eastern and Western world view
has had an impact on the philosophical outlook on
the social, political, educational, economical,
religious and physical design of each environment. One source puts it:

It is not, therefore, by accident that
the Polar igloos, South Sea grass huts,
American plains, 'Indian' lodges,
Chinese pagodas and Congolese mud huts
all share basically the same similarities and all the social, political and
economic institutions erected by traditional men reflect the symmetry ever
present in nature...All Eastern culture
is highly symmetrical.[36]

Thus, it is not by accident that the physical design of the Western world's building structure is
horizontal and vertical (linear) and the structure of the Eastern physical world is circular.
By the same token, it is purposeful that the
Africans, Native Americans and other Eastern cultures sat in circles, danced in circles and con-
ducted their ceremonies in circles.

In traditional Africa, decision-making is conduc-
ted by the elders of the community "who sit and
argue until they agree" and reach consensus. At
the same time, it is purposeful that the physical
arrangement of chairs in classrooms, churches and
meeting places in the Western culture are arranged vertically or horizontally with everyone
facing the speaker. Inherent in this seating ar-
rangement is the placement of superior and subor-
dinates, symbolizing a linear and dichotomous
structure. In contemporary America it is considered more humane to conduct classes and semi-
nars with the chairs arranged in a circle because

54

everyone is able to have face-to-face contact and the "authority" of speaker is lessened.

In the Western world, the structure of the bureaucracy and decision-making is linear and compartmentalized. The work force is broken up into apprentice-master, craftsman-worker supervisor, director and president, with the line of communication being such that the person at the lower end of the continuum cannot communicate directly with the individual at the top of the hierarchy. Instead, communication must be directed through the hierarchy at every level. In decision-making the power rests within the hierarchy of the linear structure with the person highest on the scale possessing the greatest power, and each person in a descending order possessing a lesser degree of power. In traditional Eastern cultures power generally rests in the hands of the elders and continuously revolves (circular) from one generation to the next with everyone having the opportunity to be a decision maker.

On the other hand, the concept of majority rule is compartmentalized at the top of the linear hierarchy in the Western cultures, with minority concerns secondary. This is different in the Eastern culture where the concept of consensus and unity in decision-making prevails and is circular in dimension. The concept of majority rule is placed high on the linear scale in the Western world view while the concerns of consensus and unity are minimized.

The Eastern/African philosophical statement that best captures the African/Eastern ideology is "I am because we are; therefore, I am", and the epitomy of European/Western ideology is "I think; therefore, I am." The implication of the philosophy "I am because we are; therefore, I am" suggests oneness. It further suggests that the survival of an individual is intricately tied into the lives of other members of the society.

On the other hand, "I think; therefore, I am" places the individual at the center of the universe with "individualism" at the linear hierarchy over all else. This statement suggests that one can survive alone without human contact or reinforcement from other humans, yet this is scientifically inaccurate.

The relevance of the Eastern and Western world view upon the impact of the theoretical foundation for social work with Indians, Blacks, Puerto Ricans, Mexican-Americans and other People of Color may best be dramatized in statements from the Native-American perspective:

>Probably no other people in the United States are so misunderstood as the (minorities of the Third World) American Indian. Probably no other people have had so many myths woven about their way of life. Misinterpretation of Indian thinking, customs, and attitudes consistently and continually arise and spread. Myths about Indians are wide in range, from such prosaic subjects as every day food preferences to philosophical and religious tenents. One or more of these myths about the first Americans has influenced the ideas of almost everyone, Indian and non-Indian alike.[37]

The author further solidifies the above position by stating:

>For example, the concept of 'social work intervention' may be consistent with much of the white man's culture, but it diametrically opposes the Native American's cultural concept....[38]

Such comments as the ones stated above are articulated by many Third World minority scholars from many perspectives, such as the following statement from the Puerto Rican perspective:

In terms of a common sense example of relevance to our topic, we are arguing that a particular counseling program designed to deal with a specific type of problem might be highly successful with Chicanos, moderately successful with Cubans, and of only limited success with Puerto Ricans because of subcultural differences across groups.[39]

Mexican-American comments on the impact of World view and culture on social work intervention and People of Color are as follows:

...if we know the cultural elements that determine the structure of the Mexican-American family, we could be effective in the problem solving process in this particular aspect of the life experience of the Mexican-American.[40]

The many similarities and commonalities existing in the culture of People of Color coupled with the impediments of the Western world view theory-base for social casework strongly suggest that the social work profession must become sensitive and relevant to the culture and world view of Black Americans, Puerto Ricans, Mexican-Americans, Indians and other Third World minorities. Some of the commonalities among People of Color are as follows:

Each culture places a high regard and respect for the elders of their communities, oftentimes as mentors and decision makers in their families. This is an extension of early tradition where the elders played significant roles in the community.

Each culture maintains an extended family relationship, which includes family members as well as nonfamily members.

Each culture continues to maintain a belief in the workings of supernatural forces, which cause evil as well as good in their day-to-day lives. They have not completely separated the spiritual from the material in that oftentimes they see certain rituals as being able to resolve the misfortune they face.

Each culture has significantly integrated man and nature in that there is more of a humanistic tolerance and acceptance of other ethnic groups and races (including whites). There is the philosophy that 'I am because we are; therefore, I am' in contrast to the Western view that 'I think; therefore, I am.'

In one form or another each minority group member from the Eastern world view perspective has adopted the circular logic of 'what goes around comes around' and 'you are going to reap what you sow' as the philosophy that guides his/her behavior and teaches those principles to his/her children. Inherent in the notion of 'what goes around comes around' is the view that you should be careful how you treat other people in the **circle** of humans because the same treatment may revolve back to you. The principles are hidden in the philosophy of 'I am because we are; therefore, I am.'

HISTORICAL DYNAMICS OF SOCIAL CASEWORK
WITH
PEOPLE OF COLOR

Historically, the dynamics of social casework with People of Color began with the white worker and Black client. One of the very first articles addressing race and the essence of psychotherapy with People of Color was written by Viola Bernard in her essay "Psychoanalysis and Members of Minority Groups." According to Viola Bernard:

> For many reasons patients of greater diversity in the terms of class and costs are undertaking psychoanalytic treatment. Similarly, cultural diversity is increasing for the analytic trainee population. Meanwhile, as we know, psychoanalytic theory is concerning itself more and more with the study of ego functioning, with consequently increased emphasis on deeper understanding between social reality and personality development and functioning. These desirable developments render it timely that the psychoanalyst as therapist and investigator take into account his own cultural position and social attitude, conscious and unconscious, with particular reference to prejudice.[41]

The author went on further to point out that:

> The respective subcultural groups to which patient and analyst belong can be regarded as constituting a special dynamic factor of the analytic situation and as such can be provocative of counter-transference.[42]

The major concerns during the initial stages of a therapeutic relationship with People of Color focused on the worker exploring conscious and/or unconscious feelings and attitudes of racial prejudices inherent in self that may handicap an effective relationship with members of different ethnic and racial groups.[43] Other pioneers exploring the relevance of race and culture agreed that racial prejudices and tension in racial relationships could contribute to difficulties in interaction, communication, rapport and trust,

59

which are significant factors in effective therapy. The fact that the initial theoretical discussions on race and ethnicity focused on the white therapist and the Third World client may be related to the lack of Third World therapists during that time. Research data revealed other important factors:

> Of particular importance to the practice of social caseworker and the white therapist/Black client relationship is a study that was conducted by Luna B. Brown in 1949 on the differences in worker and client and its impact on the therapeutic relationship.[44] It was concluded after the study that a 'denied feeling' against Negro clients may underlie a good deal of success of some white workers with Black clients. The reason for the 'denial feeling' or 'blind spot,' as referred to at the time of the report, may be contributed to (a) lack of association with Negroes (b) learned an ingrained attitude toward them (Black) and (c) 'a personal need to find security through a sense of racial superiority.' She further concluded that the issue of race should only be brought up in the therapeutic relationship 'when appropriate' and the experience of the worker compensated for factors of race.[45]

Given the few available Third World professional therapists of the mid-twentieth century coupled with the few Third World clients, most of whom were Black, much of the literary focus was placed on dynamics between the white case worker and the Black client. As the 1960's emerged and the number of Third World professional therapists and clients increased, there developed an emphasis on the Black worker/client relationship. In view of the Black worker/white client relationship, one author points out:

60

It is interesting that most of the literature concerns the Negro client and the white social workers. It is likely that the Negro is often thought of in terms of being a client and that this preconception, therefore, establishes this paucity. Relatively little has been written about the problem of a Negro social worker with a white client.[46]

The unavailability of literature on this subject is undisputed, and there may be some authenticity to the conclusion by the author above that Black workers are viewed as clients. This is of particular importance given the insensitivity of white publishing firms toward Black articles and manuscripts. Other factors that may have contributed to this fact during the early 1950's were:

Lack of professional journals in Social Work.

Few, if any People of Color on the editorial boards of professional social work journals.

Evaluation of manuscripts by white editors who may be over-sensitive to the Black therapist's theoretical assumptions and observations.

Needless to say, the case illustrations that emerged in social work practice during the 60's, 70's and 80's provided extensive data for analysis and interpretation. However, as we look at the case illustrations closely, we will find that most of the same variables operating in the white therapist/Black client interaction and relationship are functional in one dynamic form or another in the Black therapist/white client relationship. Such dynamics can best be described as follows:

Thus separated by race, money, education, social position, power, and lack of real knowledge of and feeling for the other's life experience, the white professional and Black client come together (Black professional and white client). They face each other and are confronted with the necessity of doing something together. The reactions they may have to each other and to the situation in which they find themselves are the dynamics of the encounter with which they must cope in order to work together. In essence, both professionals and clients are what they are based upon their past experiences and the society in which they live and interact. They do not know each other; they do not trust each other. Indeed, they most probably have many feelings about each other, themselves, and their respective positions which in reality impede the development of trust and concomitant mutual honesty. First there is suspiciousness and fear between them. 'What is the other really thinking and feeling? What does he really want? What does he really mean? How much does he hate me, blame me or want to con me? How can he hurt me or take advantage of me?[47]

Given the variables of trust versus mistrust between Black worker and white client, it is conceivable that many white, as well as Black, therapists may make decisions to avoid penetration of the presenting problems in working with clients from opposite races. The white therapist may be "worried" about how he/she is coming across, how he/she is perceived and what the client "really" thinks of him/her. (The same may be true of a Black therapist with a white client.) Therefore, there may be a strong inclination on the part of the therapist to be superficial (chit-chat) and stay on the surface rather

than open up "Pandora's box" where the therapist
may have to reveal his true feelings and perceptions. So, the therapist's concern of "Will you
(the client) be able to accept me if I (the therapist) revealed myself to you," is a hindrance to
client disclosure because the therapists "don't
want to get into it." By the same token, the
"unknowingness" of the Black world may make the
white therapist feel that he/she may be inadequate or incapable of dealing with what is revealed and uncovered in the same way that the
white world of prejudice and racism may be
threatening to the Black client. Most of all,
there is a view held by the therapist that he/she
may be hurt or may inflict pain based on the
interaction. The result of such anxiety on the
part of the therapist is a deterrent to exploring
and/or penetrating areas of trust, rapport and
self-disclosure where matters of race are concerned.

Futher exploration of the Black/white worker/-
client relationship will reveal that the worker
should address the issue of race early in the
therapeutic relationship. This is not to suggest
that the worker should immediately begin penetrating or exploring the area of trust and self-
disclosure with the client during the initial
therapeutic interaction. By the same token, this
is not to suggest that the therapist should violate the right of the client to move at his/her
own pace in revealing very sensitive material as
pertinent in any given case. At the same time,
there is no passport for therapists in Black/-
white interactions to act out their fantasies in
the world of the "unknown" by encouraging their
clients to repeatedly reveal material for the
therapist's personal self-gratification. It is
necessary, however, for the therapists to recognize that both worker and client are in an anxious relationship in Black/white interaction and
at some point these anxieties must be addressed
in order to create trust. Anxieties and insecurities are decreased by the worker and client dis-
cussing the factors that may be precipitating the

anxiety rather than leaving them dormant. In fact, if the factors percipitating anxieties in the client or worker are avoided, the anxieties are increased and not decreased.

The historical foundation of social casework with People of Color reveals that the therapists' knowledge of human behavior without the considerations of race and culture oftentimes justifies and covers up many of the inadequacies of workers in relating to minorities. Another common dynamic existing between worker and client of different racial ethnic dyad is the problem of client self-disclosure. As one source puts it:

> Self-disclosure, or the unwillingness to let another person know what you think, feel, or want, is basic to the counseling process. It is especially crucial in the rapport establishing phase of the relationship because self-disclosure is the most direct means by which an individual can make himself known to another person and this is prerequisite to achieving the goals of counseling.[48]

Another factor that has emerged over the decades is open expression of angry and hostile feelings by People of Color toward the white society in response to the oppression of the "system" and the "establishment." If we look at this logically, we will come up with the following premise: The system and the establishment are dominated by whites; yet the system and the establishment are so abstract they are impossible to attack; consequently, Blacks are forced to identify white individuals as the oppressor and react to them as such.

Many psychiatrists and social scientists have attributed Black aggression to a manifestation of subconscious, self destructive forces in Black people stemming from this chronic feeling of self-denigration. Kenneth B. Clarke has even speculated that these riots are a form of Com-

feel that the role of a conforming 'banana' (a derogatory term used to describe a person of Asian ancestry who is 'yellow' on the outside but white on the inside) is too degrading. In an attempt to gain the self-respect they feel has been denied them by white society, they have banded together in an attempt to reverse the negative trend of **bananaism** among their own group. This group of individuals seem much more aware of political, economic, and social forces that have shaped their identity. They feel that society is to blame for their present dilemma and are actively challenging the establishment. They are openly suspicious of institutions, such as counseling services, because they view them as agents of the establishment.[51]

In a review of history, it is also apparent that Third World American clients are very sensitive about the barriers that language differences play in their interaction with white America's institutions and systems for receiving social services.[52]

As for the language barrier much has been written about its importance in establishing the therapeutic relationship.... This variable undoubtedly has an immeasurable effect in facilitating the task at hand.[53]

It is only through the experiences of People of Color that we can truly understand and comprehend the dynamic interplay of language differences as a barrier in the case work relationship. The ability of Blacks and others to master the use of the English language, in the minds of many, somehow corresponds to the degree of their **assimilation** into the American's values and into the American system. The premise seems to be that the better you are able to master English, the more **whitewardly** mobile you become. It is the association of the English language with superiority and other languages with inferiority that is detrimental. In essence, it is the white supremacists' ethnocentric view of the English language and American culture that is responsible for the condescension and resulting harrassment of many Third World clients who are unable to speak the English language effectively.

As Fanon puts it:

> To speak means to be in a position to use a certain syntax to grasp the morphology of this or that language, but it means above all to assume a culture, to support the weight of a civilization (for) a man who has a language consequently possesses the World expressed and implied by that language.[54]

To further support the premise of associating the English language with superiority, Fanon adds:

> The Negro of the Antilles will be proportionately whiter -- that is, he will become closer to being a real human being -- in direct relation to his mastery of the French Language.[55]

Ultimately, the battle of language is a battle of power. The old adage that "He who has the power to define determines what is," is applicable. Needless to say, the psychological damages caused to Blacks, Indians, Puerto Ricans, Mexican-Americans and other People of Color are devastating. One expert says:

> Thus many Africans do not recognize the phenomenon which takes place in their not being able to speak the English language properly. That is, the African's struggle to survive the racist language may be seen as a psychological rejection and resistance to mastering the

67

language in the same way that there are physiological antibiotics which work to prevent the admission of foreign and harmful viruses into the body.[56]

In essence, "speaking good and proper English" has become associated with becoming closer to that which is "white." Many Third World individuals feel that they have become closer to being a "real human being" in direct ratio to their mastery of the English Language. However, there may be a relationship between the Black American resistance to the English language and the negativism inherent in the English language toward People of Color. This resistance may be a prohibiting factor to the willingness of People of Color to master the English language. In many Third World minority communities, the employment opportunities are based on how well the minority member can speak Standard English.

The implications of being a member of a Third World minority group has widespread impact and influence on the individual's behavior and action.

One author states:

To be Negro in the United States today holds certain implications for any individual, no matter how little prejudice seems to have affected him personally. His relationships not only to society at large but to parents, grandparents and siblings (and social workers are fond of considering such relationships as the crux of interpersonal problems) are in some measures affected by skin color; there is indeed no interior intra-personal problem that is not influenced by how he and his predecessors as well as his peers have reacted to that fact.[57]

These roles and relationships experienced by People of Color from birth throughout adulthood will in some way shape how they function in therapy. It is the conflict derived from trying to cope with being People of Color in a predominantly white world that contributes to many difficulties in functioning and self-actualization in the American society.

TRANSFERENCE/COUNTERTRANSFERENCE
IN
INTER-RACIAL THERAPY

In the early development of social casework and the social work profession, the theory of psychoanalysis had a profound effect on the clinical frame of reference for social casework intervention skills. Such clinical foundation is rooted in much of social casework practice today. Therefore, it is necessary for a basic understanding of those concepts as we approach transference and countertransference from an inter-racial and inter-ethnic perspective.

Sigmund Freud, the Father of Psychoanalysis and composer of the dynamics involved in transference and countertransference, defines transference as:

> ...New editions of facsimilies of the tendencies and fantasies which are aroused and made conscious during the progress of the analysis, but they have this peculiarity, which is characteristic of their species, that they replace some earlier persons by the person of the physician. To put it another way: a whole series of psychological experiences are revived, not as belonging to the past, but as applying to the physician at the present moment.[58]

Greenson adds another dimension to the concept of transference when he states that transference is:

...a distinctive type of object relationship. The main characteristics are
the experience of feeling toward a
person which do not benefit that person, and which actually apply to
another. Essentially, a person in the
present is reacted to as though he were
a person in the past.[59]

Since the popularization of transference and
countertransference as a phenomena, there has developed a host of unresolved questions regarding
these concepts. The controversy on transference
in the worker/client relationship focuses on the
following concerns:

Whether transference is directly related to an unresolved Oedipal Complex
in that the Oedipus Complex is the central problem area of each client prior
to the onset of the neurosis.[60]

Whether or not transference is regres-
sive in nature, primitive in striving
and infantile in nature.[61]

Whether or not transference is strictly
a conscious and/or unconscious phenomenon. That is, whether it is a conscious coping mechanism of the client
in relationship to the therapist or
whether it is an unconscious reaction
to the therapist.[62]

Whether or not transference is dis-
placement or projection and whether it
is the significant others in the person's life who may be transferred to
the therapist or whether all persons in
the client's life may be considered.[63]

Whether or not transference is the result of anxiety provoked by the therapist,
which leads to defense coping mechanism

of the client.[64]

Whether the nature of positive and negative transference interact in its implication for psychotherapy or whether all transference is absolutely negative or absolutely postive.[65]

Whether there is any validity to the concept of transference or whether it is a defense reaction of the therapist who is unwilling to look objectively at the characteristics of his/her behavior in relationship to the client.[66]

Given all of the debates and controversy on transference, there appears to be consensus of the following:

The client oftentimes irrationally views the therapist as persons of significant others in his/her past and reacts to the therapist accordingly.

It is the role of the worker to utilize his/her relationship skills in assisting the client to overcome the transference and, thereby, resolve the underlying psychological difficulties.

Negative transference is the client's unrealistic transfer of negative characteristics onto the therapist from experiences with significant others in the past, and positive transference is the transfer of irrational positive characteristics onto the therapist from experiences with significant others in the past.

It is through the effective use of transference that the therapist is able to pinpoint many of the major difficulties inherent in the client's psychological problems.

71

> The reality base of the client's response to the therapist's behavior is not transference but may provoke a countertransference reaction in the worker.

> The therapist must be cognizant of his/her reactions to the client that may result into countertransference.

Countertransference is another significant phenomenon in the casework therapeutic process. According to Ruesch:

> Countertransference is transference in reverse. The therapist's unresolved conflicts force him to invest the patient with certain properties which bear upon his own past experiences rather than to constitute reaction to the patient's actual behavior. All that was said about transference, therefore, also applies to countertransference, with the addition that it is the transference of the patient which triggers into existence the countertransference of the therapist.[67]

It is apparent from the definition above that therapists may have years of supervised experience and academic training but are still subject to countertransference reactions. Erwin Singer in his book, Key Concepts in Psychotherapy, states that:

> Countertransference is understood as a development highly analogous to transference. It is assumed that its appearance is governed by essentially the same processes, drives and tendencies which authors posit in their respective explanation of the transference phenomenon.[68]

As the debate continues on the nature of transference in psychotherapy, there is a corresponding debate on the use and management of countertransference. Most authorities seem to agree that:

Countertransference exists.

Countertransference on the part of the therapist is usually provoked by the transference reaction of the client or produced by unresolved anxieties in the therapist.

The recognition of countertransference by the therapist may be utilized as a therapeutic component in the therapeutic relationship.

Remaining unchecked, countertransference reaction on the part of the therapist will cause further deterioration to the client.

Countertransference is the result of a lack of self-awareness on the part of the therapist or the therapist's reluctance to know and/or learn something about him/her self.

On the dynamics of transference and countertransference, the following questions must be asked. What is the relationship of the classical phenomena of transference and countertransference on inter/intra-racial and ethnic therapeutic relationships that must be confronted? Is there any relationship or significance of transference and countertransference that must be understood in relationship to race and culture? Is race and ethnicity a factor to be considered in transference and countertransference or should caseworkers deny race and ethnicity of worker and client as significant in transference and countertransference? Is the classical definition of transference and countertransference applicable to differences in race and ethnicity of therapist and client? These and other questions must be analyzed and addressed in order to understand the relevance and significance of differences in ethnicity and race of caseworker and client.

The relevance of transference and countertransference in inter-racial relations is described as follows:

> Transference is especially knotty in the white-black dyad, because the black client brings to the relationship intense notions derived from his experience with and feelings toward whites in general, as Greenson points out. The Negro membership in an ostracized subcultural group tends to lead to certain habitual ways of relating initially to a member of the majority group....This is particularly true today.
>
> Not only because Blacks still experience discrimination, insult, segregation, and the threat of violence, but also because they have become more sensitive and less adjusted to these affronts to human dignity. To them, the current problems and conflicts have much more significance than those in the past.[69]

Because transference is traditionally viewed as a response of the client to a worker in the present in a manner he/she has responded to a significant other in the past, the question on the relevance of current conflicts existing between inter-ethnic and racial minorities' relations creates a new dimension. Much of the dynamics that social caseworkers may attribute to an unconscious transference phenomenon in an inter/ethnic professional relationship may be the client's conscious reaction to the current tensions existing in interracial relations. Above all, this requires that the worker must develop self-insight and self-awareness into his/her own prejudices as they may affect his/her behavior and action in the therapeutic process.

It is detrimental to the casework process for the worker to inappropriately label current reactions of the client to deepseated transference phenomena when they are a conscious reaction to the current racial climate in the community or in therapy. In such instances, the worker focuses on the assumed, unresolved unconscious drives of the client as the core of the problem and will completely avoid the reality of the client's response. The worker's focus on unconscious causes for the client's behavior labeled as transference may be defined by the client as a defense mechanism of the worker. Secondly, there is a criticism that the social theory of psychoanalysis as actualized through transference places the blame of the client's psychopathology onto the client and deletes the current social system's impact on the individual. Such a disposition on the part of the social casework practitioner prohibits the understanding of the dynamics that current conflicts might play in inter-ethnic relations.

Consequently, social caseworkers of all racial and ethnic composition appear to be caught in an ambivalent situation in working with People of Color, but the difficulties are more paramount between white workers and People of Color. As one source puts it:

> While some white analysts seem compelled to overemphasize the effects of being Negro on their patient's personality difficulties, others have an apparent need to deny and sidestep any such effects altogether. Both overemphasizing and sidestepping seem fallacious in that they reflect a preconceived bias on the part of the analysts who should, instead, themselves be guided by what the material reveals.[70]

75

Continuing discussion on the role of the worker-minority client relationship, the author also states:

One of the most disastrous results of too much race consciousness on the part of the analyst, for whom his patient's skin color obscures his view of the whole man, is his proneness to interpret too much in terms of racial conflicts and thereby deprive the patient of thoroughly reaching and working through whatever his basic difficulties may be. The analyst may thus unwittingly ally himself with the patient's resistance in failing to grasp the unconscious defensive uses to which the Negro patient may put race prejudice. On the other hand, the analyst's blinding himself to the racial factor may also play into the patient's resistance as well as deny some of the social realities of his current existence. Some white analysts stress the defense among their Negro patients of unrealistic denial of the psychological consequences of discrimination. While doubtless this occurs, it would seem dangerous and fallacious, in the aim of overcoming this defense, for analysts to perpetuate a new form of racial stereotype -- the psychoanalytic stereotype -- i.e., the Negro personality whose frustrated hostility toward whites must always automatically continue his central conflict and the core of his personality organization. Negroes, struggling against the standard racial stereotypes, are understandably alarmed by the threat of such a sophisticated new version of racial stereotypes, under the aegis of psychodynamics.[71]

The author concludes by highlighting other important dynamics involved in the worker/minority client relationship.

> Both attitudes correspond to two rather frequently met defense patterns on the part of Negro patients -- 'All my problems are due to unfair racial discrimination,' i.e., the good excuse defense, and 'None of my problems have anything to do with being Negro and you're prejudiced if you think color made any difference in my life,' i.e., the magic denial defense.[72]

In spite of the many difficulties inherent in the worker/client relationship with People of Color, there are those who see racial and ethnic differences as a catalytic effect upon the treatment process relating to transference. As one resource states:

> Racial differences may have a catalytic effect upon the analytic process and lead to a more rapid unfolding of core problems.

> The catalytic effect of the analyst's race upon the development of transference occurs when the racial stereotypes are concerned with the same effects and conflicts as the transference.[73]

Although much of the discussion on the dynamics of the casework relationship has focused on workers and clients of different racial and ethnic groups, there are many problems inherent in worker/client relationships of the same ethnic and racial group. The literature on transference and countertransference between worker and client of the same ethnic and racial group, however, is inadequate. Some of the variables on the part of the worker affecting the transference/countertransference interaction between members of the same race and ethnicity are as follows:

Worker denial of identification with in-group ethnic/racial consciousness.

Worker over-identification with in-group ethnic/racial consciousness.

Class and status differences between therapist and client.

Worker's view of clients within his/her minority group as low status.

Worker's view of relationship with clients within his/her minority group as an ego boost to his/her own identity.

Worker's correlation of working with minority client within the same ethnic/racial group as the solution to all the difficulties that his/her minority group faces.

Worker's identification of self as being the only one who can help such minority because he/she is a member of the same group.

Worker's view that 'I am the model' by having demonstrated 'I have made it,' and the client should adopt his/her mode of behavior if he/she is to make it.

Worker's attempt to compensate for the client's station in life compared to his/her own.

The following attitudes and disposition on the part of the client with a worker of the same ethnic and racial group may provoke countertransference in the therapist.

Client's view of the therapist as having 'sold out' to the white society due to his/her role in white society as part of the establishment.

Client's view of the therapist as being unable to understand, empathize or appreciate the **Black, Red, Yellow,** experience due to social and class differences.

Client's accusation that the therapist is attempting to convert him/her into the middle class standards and life styles of the therapist.

Minority client's view of the minority therapist as inferior or incapable of being able to help.

A few of the important factors that may have an impact on the transference and countertransference transaction between social caseworkers and People of Color are:

There is a negative impact of social and economic discrimination on the personality structure of Third world minorities.[74]

Suspicion and distrust of Third World minorities toward whites is a normal consequence of victimization by prejudice.[75]

Existence of a 'moral uneasiness' in workers who experience individual and collective guilt causes many workers to live in a constant state of conflict with People of Color.[76]

There is a need for the removal of the barriers of segregation to alleviate the psychological damage to People of Color.[77]

There is an assumption of innate infer-

iority of Third World minority cul-
culture and intelligence.[78]

There are a host of negative stereotypes regarding social and sexual behavior of People of Color.[79]

The assignment of negative social and
psychological behavior to People of
Color as being uniquely Third World.[80]

The view that Third World minority individuals are culturally deprived and
do not have a culture.

22. Thomas Szasz. "Blackness and Madness," Yale
    Review, Yale University Press, (1970),
    p. 334.

23. Walter Ong. "World View and World as
    Event," presented at Wenner-Foundation Burg
    Warternslein-Symposium, Paper No. 41,
    August 2-11, (1968).

24. Jessie A. White. "The Concept of Culture,"
    American Anthropology, Vol. 61,
    (April, 1959), p. 227.

25. Arthur L. Smith (ed.) Language
    Communication and Rhetoric in Black America,
    (New York: Harper and Row Publishers, 1972),
    p. 323.

26. Ibid. "Expressive Language," p. 323.

27. Florence Hollis. Casework: A Psychosocial
    Therapy, (New York: Random House, 1964),
    p. 186.

28. Elizabeth Meier. "Social and Cultural
    Factors in Casework Diagnosis," Social
    Work, (July, 1959), p. 16.

29. Elena Gonzales. "Role of the Chicano Folk
    Belief and Practices in Mental Health," in
    Hernadez-Haugh-Wagner (ed). Chicanos:
    Social and Psychological Perspectives,
    St. Louis: G. V. Mosby 1976), p. 264.

30. Cedric Clarke. "Black Studies on the Study
    of Black People," in Reginald Jones (ed.)
    Black Psychology, (New York: Harper and Row
    Publishers, 1972), p. 9.

31. Winthrop Jordan. White Over Black,
    New York: Penguin Books, Inc., 1968), pp. 1-
    3.

32. Hugh Butts. "White Racism: Its Origin,
    Institution and the Implication for

Professional Practice for Mental Health,"
International Journal of Psychiatry, Vol. 8,
No. 6 (December 1969), p. 917; Ethel
Pearson, "Racism: Evil or Ill,"
International Journal of Psychiatry, Vol. 8,
No. 6, (December 1969), p. 929.

33. John O. Killens. _Black Man's Burden_,
New York: Pocketbook, a Division of Simon
and Schuster, Inc., 1965), p. 9.

34. Charles Frye. "The Psychology of the Black
Experience: A Jungian Approach," (Journal
unknown) p. 12.

35. Reginald Jones (ed). _Black Psychology_,
"Black Studies of the Study of Black
People," (Cedric Clarke) Harper and Row
Publishers, (1972), p. 2.

36. Charles Frye. "The Psychology of the Black
Experience, A Jungian Approach," (Journal
unknown) p. 12.

37. Herbert H. Locklear. "American Indian
Myths," _Social Work_, (May 1972), p. 72.

38. Ronald G. Lewis & Man Keung Ho. "Social
Work with Native Americans," _Social Work_,
(September, 1975), p. 381.

39. Rene A. Ruiz and Amado M. Padilla.
"Counseling Latino's," _Personnel and
Guidance Journal_, (March, 1977), pp. 401-
402.

40. Marta Sotomayor. "Mexican-American
Interactions with Social Systems," _Social
Casework_, (May, 1971),p. 316.

41. Viola Bernard. "Psychoanalysis and Members
of Minority Groups," _Journal of the American
Psychoanalytic Association_, Vol. 1, (1953),
p. 257.

42. Ibid. p. 257.

43. J. A. Kennedy. "Problems Posed in the
    Analysis of Negro Clients," Psychiatry,
    Vol. 15, (1952).

    Inabel Lindsay. "Race as a Factor in the
    Casework Role," Journal of Social Casework,
    Vol. XXVIII, (March, 1947).

44. Luna B. Brown. "Race as a Factor in
    Establishing a Casework Relationship,"
    Social Casework, (March, 1950) Vol. XXXI,
    No. 3.

45. David R. Burgest (ed). "Minority Group
    Separatism: Implication for Social
    Treatment," in Social Work Practice with
    Minorities, (Metuchen: Scarecrow Press,
    1982).

46. Jerome Cohen. "Race as a Factor in Social
    Work Practice," in Roger R. Miller (ed).
    Race, Research and Reason: Social Work
    Perspective (New York: National Association
    of Social Workers, 1979), pp. 99-113.

47. Alex Gitterman and Alice Schaeffer. "The
    White Professional and the Black Client,"
    Social Casework, Vol. 53, (May, 1972),
    pp. 280-281.

48. Clemmont E. Vontress. "Racial Differences:
    Impediment to Rapport," Journal of
    Counseling Psychology, Vol. 16, (1971),
    pp. 7-13.

49. Alvin F. Poussaint. "A Negro Psychiatrist
    Explains the Negro Psyche," New York Times
    Magazine, (August 20, 1967), p. 1.

50. Bertram P. Karon. The Negro Personality,
    (New York: Springer Publishing Co., Inc.,
    1958), P. 45.

51. Derald Wing Sue and Stanley Sue.
     "Counseling Chinese-American," The
     Personnel and Guidance Journal, Vol. 50,
     (1952), p. 641.

52. Ignacio Aquilar. "Initial Contacts with
     Mexican-American Families," Social Work,
     (May 1972).

     Marta Sotomayor. "Mexican American Inter-
     action with Social Systems," Social
     Casework, (May, 1971) See also John D.
     Cormican. "Linguistic issues in
     Interviewing," Social Casework,
     (March, 1978) "White Clinician: The Men's
     Burden," The Black Scholar, July-August,
     (1975).

     Sonia Badillo Ghali. "Culture Sensitivity
     and the Puerto Rican Client," Social
     Casework, Vol. 58, No. 3, (October, 1977).

53. Manuel Miranda and Harry L. Kitano.
     "Barriers to Mental Health Services: A
     Japanese-American and Mexican-American
     Dilemma," in Hernandez-Haugh-Wagner (ed),
     Chicanos: Social and Psychological
     Perspectives, (St. Louis: G. V. Mosby,
     1976), p. 247.

54. Frantz Fanon. Black Skin/White Mask,
     New York: Grove Press, inc., 1967), pp. 17-
     18.

55. Ibid. pp. 17-18.

56. David R. Burgest. "Racist Use of the
     English Language," The Black Scholar
     (September - October 1973), p. 38.

57. Jean S. Gochros. "Recognition and Use of
     Anger in Negro Clients," Social Work
     Vol. 11, No. 1, (January 1966), p. 29.

58. Sigmund Freud, (1905). "Fragments of an

Analysis of a Case on Hysteria," Standard Edition, (London: The Hogarth Press, 1953), pp. 7-122.

59. R. Greenson. The Techniques and Practices of Psychoanalysis, (New York: International Universities Press, 1968), pp. 30-31, pp. 151-152.

60. R. W. White. "Motivation Reconsidered: The Concept of Competence,: Psychological Review (1959) Vol. 66 pp. 297-333;
I. Hendrix "Instinct and the Ego During Infancy," Psychoanalytic Quarterly (1942) Vol. 11, pp. 33-58.

61. D. Rapport. "The Theory of Ego Autonomy: A Generalization," Bulletin Menninger Clinic, Vol. 22, pp. 13-35.

62. C. R. Rogers. Client-Centered Therapy, (Boston: Houghton Miffin Co., 1951).

63. H. S. Sullivan. The Interpersonal Theory of Psychiatry, (New York: W. W. Norton and Co., 1953).

64. F. Fromm-Reichmann. "Recent Advances in Psychoanalytic Therapy," in D. M. Bullard, (ed.), Psychoanalysis and Psychotherapy, (Chicago: University of Chicago Press, 1959).

65. F. Fromm-Reichmann. Principle of Intensive Psychotherapy, (Chicago: University of Chicago Press, 1950).

66. Thomas Szasz. The Myth of Mental Illness: Foundation of a Theory of Personal Conduct, (New York: Hoeber-Harper, 1961).

67. J. Ruesch. Therapeutic Communication, New York: W. W. Norton and Company, 1961), p. 175.

68. Erwin Singer. <u>Key Concepts in Psychotherapy</u>, (New York: Basic Books, Inc., 1970), pp. 290-291.

69. Clemmont Vontress. "Racial Differences: Impediment to Rapport," <u>Journal of Counseling Psychology</u>, Vol. 18, (1974), pp. 7-13.

70. Viola W. Bernard. "Psychoanalysis and Members of Minority Groups," <u>Journal of the American Psychoanalytic Association</u>, I, (April, 1953), p. 262.

71. Ibid. p. 262.

72. Ibid. p. 262.

73. Judith S. Schachter and Hugh F. Butts, "Transference and Countertransference in Inter-Racial Analysis," <u>Journal of the American Psychoanalytic Association</u>, Vol. 16, No. 4, (October, 1968).

74. Abram Kardiner and L. Ovesey. <u>The Mark of Oppression</u>, (New York: W.W. Norton and Company, 1951).

75. William H. Grier and Price M. Cobbs. <u>Black Rage</u>, (New York: Basic Books, 1968).

76. Gunnar Myrdal. <u>The American Dilemma</u>, (New York: Harper & Brothers, 1944).

77. See "The Negro in American Life and Thought: The Nadir, 1877-1901," First published in 1954 and revised in paperback as <u>The Betrayal of the Negro</u>, (New York: Collier Books, 1965).

78. Eldridge Cleaver. <u>Soul on Ice</u>, (New York: McGraw Hill Book Company, 1968). Calvin Hernton. <u>Sex and Racism in America</u>. (New York: Grove Press, 1966).

79. William H. Ryle. "The Mind of the Negro Child," <u>School and Society</u>, Vol. 1, (March 6, 1915).

80. Daniel P. Moynihan. <u>The Negro Family: The Case for National Action</u>, (Washington, D.C.: U.S. Department of Labor, Office of Planning and Research, March, 1965).

Chapter III

SOCIAL CASEWORK INTERVENTION:
WHITE WORKER/BLACK CLIENT
AND
BLACK WORKER/WHITE CLIENT
RELATIONSHIP

The white social casework practitioner, when working with Black clients, should follow these principles during the therapeutic relationship:

> The worker should explore the meaning of racial differences between worker and client early in the therapeutic relationship, whether it appears to be relevant or not.

> The worker should show a willingness to grow and learn from insight revealed and mistakes made with Black clients.

> The white worker must recognize that his/her mere physical presence in a therapeutic relationship with a Black client 'may be part of the problem.'

> The white worker must become familiar with the dynamics of racism on the psyche of Black individuals and assess the adaptive mechanism of Blacks as it may affect the worker/client interaction.

> The white workers should eliminate the traditional 'colorblindness approach,' of denying the importance and relevance of race on the therapeutic relationship.[81]

> The white worker should avoid placing the blame of his/her ineffectiveness in the therapeutic relationship on the

inadequacies of the Black client and his/her culture.[82]

In the following case illustration of **Mr. and Mrs. R.**, we will be able to see the importance and relevance of "recognizing color" in the therapeutic relationship between white worker and Black client.

Jean Gochros, in her article "Recognition and Use of Anger in Negro Clients," presents the following case illustration:

> Mr. and Mrs. R., members of a minority group, had been relief recipients for fifteen years, during which time they had several caseworkers. Mr. R., an ambulatory paranoid schizophrenic, retreated into a closet during caseworkers' visits. Even the most skilled and positive workers were unable to form more than a superficially pleasant but remote relationship with Mrs. R.. No relationship was established with the children or with Mr. R., who remained either well hidden or overtly hostile.
>
> When a student worker inherited the case for a nine-month period, his efforts proved equally futile. After some time Mrs. R. remained as polite, impassive and remote as ever, and the worker had not even met Mr. R. or the children.
>
> The possibility of the involvement of racial factors was discussed in a supervisory conference, but it was mutually agreed that since problems seemed no different than any other schizophrenic or culturally deprived nonverbal AFDC family, to introduce race for no apparent reason would be meaningless and perhaps even harmful.

Nevertheless, in one painfully silent interview the worker impulsively told Mrs. R. that he would like to bring up something he had been thinking about. In effect, he recognized discrimination toward members of Mrs. R.'s group and wondered if it had perhaps added to Mrs. R.'s problems. There was no response. The worker said he thought it must be very hard for people to have to receive help from the very group that had made life so difficult for them in the first place. He imagined that many people would wonder if their own workers were prejudiced and might be both fearful and resentful. Perhaps Mrs. R. had felt that way at times and maybe even about him. The response was a vague smile. The worker finally said that he did not mean to try to pry, but he wanted Mrs. R. to know that if she ever did have feelings that she wanted to talk over, he would try to understand and help in any way possible. He left the interview certain that his client had either not understood what he was saying, was too suspicious to care, or that he, himself, had been on the wrong track.

At the next interview, however, the whole atmosphere had suddenly changed. Mrs. R. met him at the door warmly, introduced him to the children, and initiated conversation for the first time.

Mr. R. had left his closet door ajar and peered out at the worker frequently. He finally entered the room, sat down beside the worker, and engaged him in conversation. In the same interview Mrs. R. confided her worry about her teen-age daughter, whose shyness and inability to make friends had caused her to leave school and remain in the house most of the time.   Mrs. R. eagerly accepted the worker's offer to help, and weekly interviews with the girl were soon set up.   The daughter later accepted enrollment in a teen-age section of an adult education school, where she was tested and found to have special abilities.   She did well in classes, began to make friends and to become more self-assured, and by the semester's end was seen by her worker, teacher and family as greatly improved.

Interviews with Mrs. R. remained somewhat superficial as to topic, but showed increased ease and warmth, with Mr. R. participating frequently.   Eventually Mrs. R. made her first office visit in years, to discuss her loneliness and fear of approaching neighbors not of her group.   With minimal help she was able to initiate and achieve friendships with these neighbors.[83]

It is significant to note in the "R" case that the agency had worked with this family for **fifteen long years** without any evidence of progress until the worker recognized the revelance of race by "citing discrimination" toward the client by white society and addressing the impact of the client's race on the social work relationship.   Immediately following this therapeutic interaction, "the whole atmosphere suddenly changed" and therapy progressed.

One of the major factors that must be readily recognized by the white worker is the role that overt recognition of race/ethnicity may play in the therapeutic relationship as it facilitates communication in the white therapist/Black client relationship.   The question of race/ethnicity should be explored early in the relationship "as a general rule."   This simple recognition of racial differences plays a significant role in the interaction and communication process between worker and client allowing for pertinent data to emerge in the therapeutic process. Effective communication cannot take place when the presenting problem of a client is affected by underlying relationship problems. In cases where there is a difference in the race/ethnicity of worker and client, these underlying relationship problems may be debilitating to communication and trust. By addressing the issue of race/ethnicity as it may pertain to possible difficulties in the therapeutic relationship, the worker sensitized the client to the fact that there will be no barriers in communication to the formulation of an open therapeutic interaction.

As demonstrated in the case illustration of **Mr. R.**, the simple avoidance of race created a far-reaching resistance to movement in the therapeutic relationship. The client may be angry at the way he/she is treated because of his/her color and the unwillingness or inability of the white therapist to understand or share in that anger may create barriers in the relationship. The worker should always address the question of race to highlight the possibility that, "I may be part of the problem" or "I recognize that the system and society in which we both live may present special problems to you, the client because you are Black."

The underlying dynamics of a worker's resistance to introduce the variable of racial differences on the impact of the therapeutic relationship may reveal a fear and anxiety on the part of some workers. Other workers may feel insecure in handling the deep-rooted feelings and emotions they fear might be uncovered. On the other hand, workers may fear that the data revealed may stimulate quilt, hostility and anger in themselves or in the client and may become destructive in the therapeutic process. Yet, to underplay the relevance of race/ethnic differences in social casework by denying the issue of race is a means of supporting a superficial non-productive relationship between worker and client. The avoidance of race may handicap the worker's potential for deeply penetrating the client's more subtle problems. Caseworkers should be able to learn from the case of **Mrs. R.** and see that it should not take **fifteen unsuccessful years** of casework therapy before addressing the relevance of racial/ethnic differences in the casework relationship.

Many white therapists fail to address the implication of racial/ethnic difference with the client for fear that the barriers and reactions by the client may be greater than the problems presented if the issue of race was not considered. On the other hand, a white caseworker should not overdramatize an identification with Black clients and provoke distrustfulness and suspiciousness on the part of the client to question the worker's motives and authenticity. Such behavior on the part of the worker may create stereotypes that suggest to the client that the worker is being manipulative and cannot be trusted. This negative reaction on the part of the client may interfere with the therapeutic relationship in that the client's distrust may generate such games as "prove to me that you are not racist." At first glance, the role of the white worker may appear to be contradictory in relationship with the minority client for the worker is being asked to acknowledge race, on the one hand, and being asked not to "overdo" it on the other hand. The solution to the white therapist's dilemma is to consider the factor of the client's race with objectivity and as he/she would explore other facets of the client's life that may impinge on the treatment process. The discussion of race-related materials should be initiated just as any other aspect of a client's life, and its relevance to therapy should be initiated and explored such as the areas of sex, health and finance.

Needless to say, any casework practitioner who

may have serious unresolved emotions and experiences in relating to ethnic minorities may be ineffective and damaging in the therapeutic process. In the same way that unresolved anxieties of the worker in such areas as sex and marital relations may adversely affect the therapeutic process, the same is true of race-related matters. The client's ability to pick up on the unresolved anxieties of the worker may be the greatest obstacle to the therapeutic process.

As we continue the exploration of the underlying dynamics involved in the white worker/Black client relationships and the significance of racial differences, it is important to caution caseworkers against unnecessary penetration and discussion on the factors of race as a means of acting out taboo and unconscious fantasies. Therefore, the caseworker must have some degree of self-awareness and self-insight regarding the helping process and solicit material only purposeful and relevant to the treatment goals.

The white caseworker must analyze his/her own emotional sensitivity to the culture of Third World minorities. In many ways social caseworkers may be better prepared to maintain objectivity and emotional stability when the problem is related to sex or other unresolved concerns than unresolved concerns related to race.

Another factor that must be considered in the white worker/Black client relationship is **repressed anger** in Black clients. As indicated in the **"R"** case, anger and hosility may be disguised through apologetic and ingratiating behavior and need not necessarily be overt. The more subtle forms of anger and hostility may go unnoticed by the white worker due to the inability of him/her to recognize the subtle psychological response of Blacks to racism. The classical reaction in the social work profession is to place blame on the client for lack of movement in therapy rather than address the inadequacies in self-awareness, sensitivity and expertise of the worker. Thus, it is often the worker's insensitivity and lack of knowledge about the dynamics of Black/white interaction, combined with the worker's assumption that the "color is unimportant in the therapeutic relationship," that is detrimental to the therapeutic relationship.

There may be white therapists who feel handicapped because "they do not know what it feels like to be Black," and they feel that this is necessary before they can develop genuine empathy with the Black client. Consequently, this perceived deficit produces anxiety in many white workers to the point that they avoid the subject of race with Black clients. On the other hand, there are Black clients who will exacerbate the situation by telling white workers that "you do not know what it means to be Black." Yet, white therapists should be supported by the knowledge-base which stipulates that it is not necessary for the therapist to experience what the client experiences in order to facilitate meaningful treatment. In other words, it is not necessary for a therapist to be married in order to work effectively with clients who have marital problems, nor is it necessary for a worker to have been a fomer drug addict in order to work with persons who have drug problems. Therefore, it is not necessary for a white worker to experience being Black in order to be effective with Black clients. It is the task of social work practitioners to be able to thoroughly penetrate the world of the client utilizing social work skills to "see what the client sees" and "feel what the client feels." It is impossible for every therapist to have experienced problems similar to the ones presented by the clients they help. It is just as theoretically absurd for a mentally ill patient to tell a therapist that "you cannot help me because you have never had a mental illness" as it is for a Black client to simply say, "You cannot help because you do not know what it means to be Black."

A widespread phenomenon inherent in the white

worker/Black client relationship is the clients' "blaming the difficulties they face" on white society and/or criticizing the white worker for "not being able to understand because you are white." This syndrome is similar in nature to the, "You haven't experienced what I have experienced being Black, therefore, you cannot help me" syndrome.

The client's attitude of, "You can't understand because you are white," may be more widespread than recognized in that often it may be concealed and covert. Schachter and Butts experienced this factor in "Transference and Countertransference in Interracial Analysis" in the white worker/Black client relationship. According to the authors:

> At the beginning of the fourth year of his analysis, he met the young Negro professional woman he married two years later. She was presumably engaged to a very light-skinned Negro man in a position of social importance, and he both acted out his Oedipal anxieties and became aware of them in the transference. The use of color as a barrier to sexual impulses to mother was further explored since it included his picture of father, the Negro, as neither gratifying mother nor control of impulses, thereby exposing the patient to his sexual desire for mother. At the same time, he felt that he had to lose out to a light-skinned man and could win only if he associated with darker people. 'I get angry at all white people and have to think a second time.' His attempt to exempt the Jewish analyst because of similarity in minority status was confronted by the distinction between our social problems as well as his need to obliterate differences. As he grappled to understand the nature of the sexual barrier

between us, and between him and mother,
he repeatedly came back to color. In a
dream, the slow analytic train was held
up by white barriers, which represented
the analyst, who would cause the crash
and hurt the driver. Further associations were to the analyst's open and
free attitude toward color in combination to his own feelings of prejudice
against dark women. His angry self-
justification was: 'You've had a better life than I...You can afford to be
more liberal, freer of prejudice than
I...how can you understand what it is
to be a Negro in America...a bitter
thought...it's one thing to see something from the outside and another to
live within it.'[84]

As stated earlier, there is no need for a white
therapist to feel guilty or apologetic for not
having lived in the Black world and "experienced
being Black," just as it is not necessary for any
therapist to be made to feel guilty because he/
she has not experienced imprisonment or any other
conditions pertaining to a client's condition.
It is the role and resposibility of the therapist
to utilize his/her academic and professional
skills to assist the client to become a full participating and functional member of the society
and world in which he/she lives.

In addition to the above, the white therapist
must be sensitive to the fact that he/she is not
acting out his/her personal needs through stimulating guilt reactions in Third World minority
clients as a means of provoking anger and hostilities that will be redirected to the worker.
In such instances the ego needs of the worker to
be "whipped" by the client is nonproductive and
ineffective in the therapeutic process. The
worker's assumption that, "I may be part of the
problem," asserts a willingness on the part of
the worker to take risks in the relationship in
seeking a solution to the client's problem. The

overriding assumption on the part of the therapist must be that, "I do not need to experience
the pain of the client in order to work to alleviate the pain." The worker must express a
willingness to expose his/her biases to risk
growth and development in the therapeutic relationship.

There are white therapists who are too quick to
say "I understand" to Black clients in order to
demonstrate empathy and sincerity and thereby relinquish genuine concern due to feelings of guilt
and powerlessness. It is detrimental to feign
"understanding" when the worker, in fact, may not
"understand." This attitude, on the part of the
worker, creates an irresolvable situation when
the client senses that the therapist is **understanding** the "wrong thing." The **meaningless** verbalization of "I understand" may be voiced at a
juncture in the interview process where that was
not the point of understanding the client was
trying to convey. The client will see the therapist as not listening, too quick to provide comfort where not wanted or needed, and lacking intellectual and emotional depth, sincerity and
honesty. The following factors should be realized in the white worker/Black client relationship in regard to the dynamics discussed above:

> The Black client's anger at the way
> he/she is treated by white society may
> lead to self-abnegation, low self-
> esteem, hostility and apologetic be-
> havior toward the white worker, which
> is destructive to the therapeutic rela-
> tionship if it goes unnoticed.

> The white worker must recognize that
> he/she may never be totally free of
> racial prejudice and biases but should
> avoid the dynamics of trying to "prove
> that he/she is free of racial
> prejudice."

> The white worker must become familiar

with the dynamics of white supremacy/
Black oppression on the psyche of
Blacks as it may pertain to the interaction between white worker and Black
client.

The white worker must become familiar
with the dynamics of white supremacy/
Black oppression on the psyche of
whites as it may affect the interaction
of the white worker/Black client relationship.

The white worker must recognize the
client's possible assimilation of the
values and symbols in the American
society as to "what black isn't" and
"what white is" as it may pertain to
the dynamics of the white worker/Black
client relationship.

Other dimensions of the relevance in taking risks
and exploring material presented by the client
that may have significance to the racial and cultural difference of worker and client are exposed
in the **Margo Case.**

Margo is a sixteen-year old pregnant
girl living in a home for unwed
mothers. She was seen in weekly interviews by the staff social worker for a
variety of problems, including a chao-
tic family situation, the need to make
critical decisions about her life with
a new baby she was determined to keep,
and a poor self-image which severely
reduced her willingness to perceive
herself as anything but a victim.
During one of the weekly session, the
social worker remarked that she had
seen the mobile that Margo was making
in the crafts class:

Social worker: It is really lovely
what you are able to do with those tin

98

cans, empty spools, and a few scraps of ribbon and felt. I think it will be just lovely over your baby's crib!

Margo: Humph! (Scowls and turns to look at the pictures on the wall.)

Social worker: What's the matter, Margo? You don't like your work?

Margo: (Still looking at the wall.) I just did it because Miss Cohen said I had to do something. I'm not putting any ole tin cans over my baby's bed! (Turns around and glares at social worker.)

Social worker: I should have realized that it would be important to you to have new things for your baby...store-bought things! You know, I did put a mobile made by one of the girls over my baby's bed three years ago. But that just makes what you just said that much more important. You know why?

Margo: (Shakes head no.)

Social worker: It's because no matter how much I hate it or you may hate it, we do live in different worlds. So I can live in my world and not know how much you and other black girls want brand new, store-bought things for your baby; and you can live in your world and not know how much a lot of people in my world care about handmade things.

Margo: I see all those pictures of white folks and their babies in the magazines and I don't see no hand-me-downs! Everything is new!

Social worker: But that's it. Margo! It's in the magazines like that because

99

they are trying to sell you new things. It's all selling. And I'm not saying that new is not good. I just don't want you to think that I am praising something you're making for your baby because I think that is all you ought to have! I think Black people should have what they like just like white people should have what they like!

Margo: Seems to be that Blacks have to take just what they can get.

Social worker: All Blacks?

Margo: Well, most I know!

Social worker: Well, let's see what we can do about seeing to it that Margo doesn't fall into that 'most' category. If some don't, then let's make sure that Margo is in that category. How about that?

Margo: (Smiles.) Right on![85]

As we analyze this case illustration of **Margo**, we will find a rather complex situation involving the dynamics when therapist is white and client is Black. First of all, the therapist responds to the client with a candid and genuine observation that is received by the client as condescension and/or white paternalistic behavior. The client reacts and responds negatively to the perceived paternalistic attitude of the white therapist based on her view that whites are different and she (client) "wanted the same thing for her child that whites wanted for their children." The worker handled the case exceptionally well by further exploring the meaning of the dialogue without responding with guilt or anger to the client's perception of her comment. Several things could possibly have happened other than illustrated, and a few of them are as follows:

The therapist could have questioned her own initial sincerity and genuineness in face of the negative response and developed a guilt reaction.

The therapist could have become defensive about being perceived as being part of the privileged society.

The therapist could have experienced guilt for provoking such a response in the client and reacted by feelings of powerlessness and helplessness.

The therapist could have experienced guilt about being able to provide for her child while the client was unable to provide for hers.

The worker's genuine statements and observations could have appeared superficial and insincere by the client creating more destruction to the relationship.

The therapist could have denied that the issue of race had any relevance to the discussion at all and moved to another topic.

The white worker in the **Margo** case pursued her own genuine and sincere concern to the point of establishing a meaningful dialogue with the client. At the same time, the worker further supported her initial authentic response by pointing out the relevance of her comment in spite of the client's perception that the worker held a "privileged position" in society. Yet, the worker supported the right of the client to want those things she perceived as valuable and worthy for herself, while at the same time supporting the authenticity of her observation and the ego strength in the client.

The case illustration of **Margo** dramatizes the

proper and adequate approach a white therapist may use with manifested material of racial overtones affecting understanding, communication and the cultural variables in the white therapist/ Black client interaction. In both cases of **Mrs. R** and **Margo** the mere discussion and elaboration on the issue of race facilitated the relationship and brought about a deeper emotional bond between worker and client. The white worker must be openly prepared to deal with such confrontations in relationships with Black clients and must be willing to explore the subject of ethnic values and prejudice generated by the client, while at the same time being ready and willing to take a risk in the dialogue. The major point to consider is that the issue of race can never be overlooked when the therapist is white and the client Black. Historically, one of the assumptions expressed is that the therapist should address the question of race only when appropriate or part of the presenting problem. This is further supported by the theoretical notion that generally a therapist should not explore areas in therapy unrelated to the presenting problem. The overriding premise appears to be that exploration of unrelated data is designed to meet the psychic "hang-ups" of the therapist with no bearing on therapy. However, the more recent position of the social work profession, as postulated by the National Association of Social Workers, is that racism and race-relations is the number one domestic mental health problem facing Black and white Americans. Therefore, such exploration should be a given and always related to the psychological factors of the therapeutic relationship.

In view of the dynamics presented, the following factors may serve as a guide to white social workers relationship with Black clients:

Factors of blackness and whiteness would not present a problem in Black-white relationships in a society free of the negative attachment to blackness.

The worker should be open and willing to take a risk, exposing anxieties in self through exploring unknown territory with client.

The therapist should not be threatened by negative transference when the patient may be hostile but should recognize the strength in the ability of the client to express strong feelings as indicative of other strong transference reactions.

The worker should recognize that mistakes and countertransference may be inevitable, but should be quick to make adjustments and utilize this information in therapy once realized.

The white therapist should not feel anxious or threatened for "not knowing" or "not understanding," but use his/her lack of understanding to demonstrate a willingness to learn.

The white therapist must be willing to seek clarification and understanding of the client's experience rather than assuming the posture of "I understand."

The white therapist should not be fearful about a Black client provoking unaware areas of racism in him/her but should recognize that there may be unaware areas of racism inherent in his/her psychological structure and have the strength to use this knowledge therapeutically in the relationship.

Confidence, Trust, Self-disclosure
and Communication

The effective use of social work skills in the

case illustration of **Mrs. X** below will demonstrate some of the components of trust, communication, recognition of color and "lack of understanding" in regard to the strategies and techniques to be utilized in the white worker/Black
client relationship. This specific dramatization
is the outgrowth of several contacts between
therapist and client where there have been many
challenges and obstacles, but the factor of
racial differences was never seen as relevant by
the worker.

Worker: Mrs. X. said that the only
other person she had ever talked to a
long time ago was Miss O., a social
worker, and she was different too. I
asked if she was Black or white? She
said she was white, then stopped to
think and said, 'I'd never have believed I could talk like this to a
white person.' She said that the way
white people treated colored people
made her angry. She said it made her
angry that she had to call white ladies
'Miss' and they called her 'Girl' or
'Frances.' She said, 'If you're white,
you're right, if you're Black, stay
back.'

I said that Blacks did have a pretty
bad deal in America and I would expect
her to be angry and bitter. She said
life was difficult for a Black person
and the whites never let them pick
themselves up. She added that mixed
marriages made her furious because it
was 'like the Black needed the white to
get ahead.' She commented that it just
infuriated her to see an interracial
couple in the street. I asked her why
she felt so strongly about it, as if it
were a personal insult? Mrs. X.
replied, 'Listen, it is an insult. My
mother looked white and I was the Black

child of the white mother and that was a horrible feeling.'

She began talking about herself and how she had never had a break in life. Then she said, 'Colored people never get much...no decent jobs, no education, nothing.' I said I knew it was very rough to be Black in America. She said, 'It's rougher than you could know, you just can't imagine.' I said, 'I guess you're saying I really can't know how it is, how it feels, what it's like to be Black because I'm white.' She said that was true and that the Black people had it worse than any others; they just received a rotten deal from the whites.

I said, 'I'm one of the whites; does it bother you sometimes that I have more than you, that I can't even begin to know how life is for you?' She said, 'No, it doesn't bother me, that's life.' Then she paused and said, 'Yes, it does bother me, it bothers me a great deal. The whites can do anything and get away with it, but let a Black man or a Black child make a slip and they get the works!'

She continued, 'And you know the worse part is when the northern whites make like they care, and we know they don't. At least, in the South, they're honest; they hate us and they say it.' I said, 'I guess I fit in here too; I am one of the whites who acts as though she cares, and you're not sure if I don't hate you.' She shrugged and we were both silent. I said it was hard to get that out and how we felt uncomfortable, but it was good that we had made a start in talking about this subject... her feelings about being Black and my

being white did matter, and so did my
feelings, and we should try to share
them.[86]

This case illustration highlights the significance of race initiated by the worker asking the
client if the "other therapist being referred to
was white or Black." The white therapist could
have very easily minimized the significance in
the race of the other worker as being unimportant. However, by recognizing the relevance of
race in former relationships of client, the
therapist raised the question. The key factor to
be understood in this interaction is the therapist's effective use of self as a reflective tool
involving risk to elicit feelings about the interaction in the relationship. The comment, "I
am one of the whites and does it bother you sometimes that I **(may)** have more than you?" Such an
approach is necessary if the therapeutic interaction between worker and client is to be effective. The therapist and client will not be able
to proceed beyond the racial variable to reach
the presenting problem if the factors associated
with racial overtones are not uncovered.

The therapist goes further in this case illustration to say, "I guess I **(may)** fit in there too, I
am one of the whites who **(may)** act as though she
cares, and you're **(may not be)** not sure whether I
do. Maybe you are not even sure if I don't hate
you." This kind of risk taking, sensitivity to
the client's feelings, environment and circumstances, is necessary in Black/white interactions. As noted, the client was able to ventilate hostilities toward the white world directly to the therapist in the interpersonal relationships. The white therapist did not person-
alize this data and respond subjectively. Many
white therapists may fear this level of interaction and, therefore, avoid the issue of race.
Nonetheless, the concealed attitudes of the
client may be a deterrent to the therapeutic process unless the worker is able to bring this data
out in the open. Oftentimes, the repressed anger

of the client toward the white world projected to the therapist may be more destructive to the relationship in nonverbal/covert ways than it could possibly be if ventilated and discussed. Yet, the therapist may not be at all certain of where the interview will lead and may fear the unresolved anxieties that might surface in the exploration. It is only through a willingness to risk, explore and stick with the difficult challenges as demonstrated in the case of **Mrs. X** that effective therapy can take place.

A therapist's anxiety about increasing self-insight around the issue of race may be a major contributor to ineffective communication in the Black/white interaction. As in the case of **Mrs. X,** there appeared to be no certainty of how the dialogue might go between worker and client after the opening of sensitive racial material. A brief interaction between worker and client is by no means a resolution to the deep emotional feelings experienced between worker and client on the subject of race. By the same token, a single encounter may serve as an impetus to developing more authenticity in the relationship as the case progresses.

To elaborate further on the competence of the white therapist in the case of **Mrs. X,** the therapist did not limit her therapeutic approach to recognizing and highlighting the strengths in the client's willingness to ventilate. She could have voiced her discomfort, if she had any, about dealing with racial content. She could have postponed the dialogue by expressing a desire to discuss the matter at another time. Instead, the therapist acknowledged the pain involved in the transaction they both were experiencing. On the other hand, the worker may have made it easier on **Mrs. X.** by showing her the relationship between the pain she experienced in this area of dialogue and pain experienced in other areas of therapy in the past, if applicable.

Another sensitive area of concern is for the white

therapist to be confronted with being among the
"privileged society" and thereby being a perpetu-
ator or recipient of racism benefiting from Black
oppression as in the case of **Margo.** This makes
the dynamics of guilt, trust and self-disclosure
between white worker and Black client difficult.
The white therapist may very well deny being a
participant in the "privileged society" and may
justify this by describing his/her specific life
styles and difficulties denoting that there is no
difference between the two of them. On the other
hand, the therapist may acknowledge being a member of the "privileged society" but may illustrate that such does not impede his/her competence to help. The most destructive reaction by
white therapists, nonetheless, is to adopt the
view that "you (the client) are **totally responsible** for your social and psychological condition"
and/or "other minority groups made it, so why
can't you?" This perpetuates the view that the
client is a victim of his/her own circumstances.

The following techniques, principles and assumptions by the white therapist may facilitate the
therapeutic process with Black clients.

> The guilt reactions of whites toward
> racism and the treatment of Third World
> clients provoke countertransference re-
> actions that are debilitating to ther-
> apy.[87]

> The white therapist must understand the
> dynamics involved in being associated
> with a white supremacist race and its
> impact on countertransference and trans-
> ference.

> The therapist must recognize that he/
> she is not "helping the entire Black
> race" but is only helping one individu-
> al when he/she helps a Black client.

> The white worker must accept and view
> the Black client as a unique individual
> rather than as a mere reflection or
> stereotype of the "Black race."

This analysis of the white therapist's encounters
with Black clients regarding trust, self-
disclosure and guilt with the Black client continues with the case illustration of **Mr. T.**:

> A twenty-four-year-old Black man re-
> cently released from a mental hospital
> attends an outing arranged by his day
> treatment center. He only occasionally
> joins in the group's activities, but he
> does engage in a conversation initiated
> by one of the counselors, a young,
> bright, white woman, deeply conscious
> of injustice to Blacks. She has read
> about such experiences and is in no
> small way eager to even the score. As
> the conversation proceeds the Black
> patient talks of his visions, filled
> with aggression and violence. He is
> certain he can predict the future. As
> the group returns to the center the
> patient elects to sit beside the coun-
> selor commenting, as they pass through
> an affluent neighborhood, that the
> people who live there 'sure have it
> good,' and adding, 'what would be so
> bad about blowing it up? Everybody
> would sure call me a bad boy then.' It
> is white guilt that keeps the counselor
> from a helpful response. Instead she
> reports that neither she nor any white
> has the right or the capacity to inter-
> vene, only a Black therapist can be of
> help. Yet this Black man's controls
> are tenuous, his impulses overwhelming.
> He is not just putting the counselor
> on, although there may be some of that;
> he desperately needs the strength to
> control impulses as he takes his first
> faltering steps back into the community.

White guilt denied him the help he needed.[88]

This case illustration of **Mr. T.** is a classical
dramatization of ineffectiveness on the part of
the worker.   The outcome of this dramatization
must be compared with the previous two illustrations where the therapist confronted the hostilities, aggression and negative reactions of
the client.   In the case of **Mr. T.**, the worker
violated all of the principles and assumptions
governing the use of self as an effective therapist in working with Blacks due to "white guilt."

Another key concept related to the white casewor-
ker/Black client relationship is self-disclosure
and unwillingness of the client to relate to a
white therapist in trust, acceptance, rapport and
mutual sharing.   Langston Hughes states it best
from the Black perspective when he stated:

> I could tell you, if I wanted to, what
> makes me what I am.   But I don't --
> Really want to -- And you don't -- Give
> a damn![89]

The case illustration of **Mrs. B.** will dramatize
other problems of self-disclosure between white
worker and Black client.

> Mrs. B. was seeking help with her mari-
> tal problem.   The color of her skin was
> very light, and she was well dressed
> and beautifully groomed.   Mr. B. was a
> graduate of the local university and
> the local public schools.   By reason of
> geography, socioeconomic status and fa-
> miliar and personal circumstances,
> Mrs. B. has escaped the grosser forms
> of prejudice and discrimination.   Her
> capacity for insight into emotional
> problems was remarkable, and she made
> an immediate, positive transference to
> the caseworker.

110

In an interview, Mrs. B. mentioned that she had once attended a (defacto) segregated school. When the caseworker attempted to pursue the subject, Mrs. B. was silent. After the worker commented on her silence, Mrs. B. replied, 'I am sitting here wondering what kind of person you really are.' Her reply could not be categorized as resistance, for it was based on a real question about the worker's attitudes and competence in regard to a problem area with which Mrs. B. was not consciously seeking help, and one in which she was not sure she could trust him. The question also indicated a breakdown of the client's unrealistic appraisal of the worker, occasioned by the positive transference, and required building into the relationship blend some opportunity for the client to make a realistic appraisal of his attitude and competence in what was obviously a problem area for her. Because her reaction was primarily ego-oriented at that point, he did not pursue an inquiry that might have jeopardized the treatment relationship.[90]

The question of trust and confidnece is of particular importance in the Black client/white therapist dynamics, with the question of "what kind of person you 'really' are" hidden deeply in the psyche of the Black client or actively verbalized to the worker. In other words, the client is asking, "Can I trust you?" Or more importantly, "Will you be able to really understand if I told you? Do you want to understand? What are your **real** feelings about me?" and, "Can I be accepted?" This is omnipresent in the minds of most Black clients during their initial and oftentimes continuous contact with white therapists irrespective of the worker's disposition toward client. The fact of the matter is that similar concerns are raised in the minds of white therapists in their relationship with Black clients.

Recognizing the inherent concerns of the "distrust" factors or what some therapists refer to as the "unknown" in the Black client, white therapists should be prepared to eliminate and/or mitigate this variable of distrust as much as possible by uncovering the factors of mistrust. As noted in the case of **Mrs. B.**, it does not matter how effective communication and interaction appear to be on the surface, there may be the existence of unknowns regarding race operatng in the client that may be unproductive in the therapeutic relationship. The common reaction of the white therapist may be similar to the reaction to the therapist in the case of **Mrs. B.** where the therapist did not regard the issue of race as important. "All appeared well" to the worker and the issue of race did not appear relevant to the presenting problem. As discussed and illustrated earlier, however, the client's and worker's repressed anxieties about race can block effective therapy even though the racial concerns may not be associated with the presenting problems.

In the case of **Mrs. B.**, the white therapist dismissed the client's racial concerns under the assumption that the racial issue was not related to the presenting problem and that the apparent positive relationship and rapport developed did not warrant exploration of those matters. However, the material uncovered by the therapist after further exploration spoke directly to the issue of race, relationship, rapport and trust. There are no guarantees that a positive relationship experienced by white therapists with Black clients is an indication of total acceptance by the client. The client's positive response may be nothing more than an "Uncle Tom" response to "get what he/she wants" from the white therapist. It may be possible that the client has manipulated the association of the presenting

problem away from race in a way to show the
therapist what he/she thinks the therapist wants
to see rather than disclose authentic feelings.
It is probable that if the concerns around self-
disclosure were an impediment in the area of
racial issues between worker and client, the same
dynamics may be operating in areas unrelated to
race. More importantly, there must be the exploration by the white therapist on the impact of
race on the relationship with Black clients. As
demonstrated in the cases of **Margo** and
Mrs. X., white therapists are capable of using
their skills to address and resolve those problems of relationship related to race if appropriately approached. In the case of **Mrs. B.**,
the therapist concluded that it was not necessary
to pursue an inquiry on the racial material revealed and justified that position under such
social work jargon that the client's reaction was
"ego-oriented" and, therefore, might jeopardize
treatment.

In regard to rapport, communication, disclosure
and trust, the literature suggests that therapists may experience the same anxieties as the
client in establishing a relationship. Therefore, it is easy to see why many white therapists
may make a conscious decision to avoid penetration of material related to race with Black
clients. The white therapist may be worried
about how he/she is coming across and perceived.
Therefore, there may be a great inclination on
the part of the white therapist to be superficial
(chit-chat) and stay on the surface rather than
open up sensitive racial concerns and reveal the
inner concern of, "Will you (the client) be able
to accept me (the therapist) if I reveal myself
to you?" Such inhibitions of the worker are a
hindrance to client disclosure because the therapist refuses to engage in open communication. By
the same token, the "unknowingness" of the Black
world may create in the white therapist a feeling
of inadequacy in dealing with what is revealed
and uncovered by the Black client. Therefore, it
may appear safe for the white worker to avoid

client disclosure in the area of race. Most of all, there may be a view held by the therapist that he/she may be hurt or may inflict further pain on the client or self due to the revelation of more materials. The results of such anxiety on the part of the therapist is a deterrent to exploring and penetrating areas of trust, rapport and self-disclosure where matters of race are concerned.

The above discussion on trust and disclosure is not to suggest that the white therapist should begin penetrating and exploring the area of trust and self-disclosure immediately in the therapeutic relationship. Neither is this to suggest that the therapist should violate the right of the client to move at his/her own pace in revealing sensitive material. At the same time, there is no passport for white therapists to deny the relevance of race and culture in therapeutic relationships with Third World minority clients. It is necessary for white therapists to recognize that both worker and client may have anxieties in the relationship, but the anxieties must be addressed in order to create a trusting environment. It is a commonly held assumption in social work practice that anxieties are decreased by the proportion in which they are addressed through discussion and increased by the degree to which they are left alone.

In conclusion, the following must be recognized by the white therapists in their casework relationship with Black clients:

Anger, hostility and apologetic behavior may be indications of distrust that may present problems of self-disclosure.

Questions of guilt, over-identification and anti-Black attitudes and emotions that may exist in self must be analyzed.

The white caseworker should not be misled by a positive transference as being
an indication that the issue of race in
unimportant.

Guilt, racial insecurities and anxieties and fear of the unknown may be the
key cause of the white caseworker's
inability to empathize with Black clients.[91]

Sexuality and Transference/ Countertransference

The practice of social casework between white
worker and Black client is more complex when the
issue of sexuality and sexual identity is involved or when there is a difference in the sexual gender of the therapist and client. Let us
look at the case of **Mr. Y.**, an unmarried male
of mixed Black and Caucasian extractions and his
transference reaction with a white woman analyst:

An unmarried man of mixed Negro and
Caucasian extraction entered analysis
at the Columbia Psychoanalytic Clinic
because of his inability to form a sta-
ble relationship with a woman, and increasing awareness of his inability to
face marriage. He was also troubled by
difficulties at work, particularly with
a woman supervisor, which had contributed to his recent loss of a job.
He was unable to express his feelings
or to tolerate the expression of
feelings by others, and appeared passive, isolated and dependent upon his
mother.

Early childhood was spent in a white
commercial neighborhood in a northern
city, living in the maternal grand-
father's home with his light-skinned
mother and father. During the depression, the family moved to Harlem. Thus,

at six, he believed that it was his dark color that necessitated the family's choice of home. At twelve to thirteen years, he was the successful vice-president of a gang because of his boxing skill, and two years later he was caught in his first serious delinquency, pilfering from the mail. After high school graduation he got a construction job and began passive homosexual activities in toilets, apparently after his mother arranged for his girlfriend's abortion. On the job he suffered a minor injury, and during the subsequent hospitalization, he applied to and was accepted by a large Negro college out of town.[92]

This is the first indication in the psychosocial background where the impact and significance of color arose in the developmental life of the client. As the case illustration reveals, the Black client's first conscious realization of the significance of color is negative. The client "believed that it was his dark color that necessitated the family's choice of a home" from an all white area to a Black area of the community. This client's view of self as the problem or the guilty victim due to color is a common experience in the lives of Black Americans. Moreover, the American socialization process of scapegoating Blacks play a key role in fostering this assumption in Americans. Needless to say, it must have been a traumatic experience at the age of six to perceive that one's parents needed to make such drastic adjustments due to one's color. There had to be a reaction of guilt for "what he was causing" his parents to do, but, more importantly, it is clear that the client had assimilated the negative definition of Blackness as perpetuated in the American society. This socialization process, no doubt, included the mass media as well as the parents of the client by the fact that they responded to the client based on their victimization by racism and prejudice.

It is the assimilation of the ingrained values and assumptions in the American society regarding "what Black isn't" and "what white is" that is responsible for many of the difficulties and conflicts in Black/white relationships and Black/white countertransference. In fact, the dynamics of racial prejudice has an impact on Black society. For example, it is a traditional saying in Black society that "a white woman treats her man better than this." In each instance, white behavior and attitudes are viewed as superior. This view of self is acted out in transference within the white therapist/Black client relationship.

Once in college, he lived with an older woman off campus and avoided both school contacts and fraternities, which were divided along color lines. He associated only with men who were appreciably darker than himself. After graduation, he returned to his mother and sporadic employment until he was encouraged by a supervisor to take up his work seriously. In his first year he was successful and well liked and, after applying for analysis, finally moved into his own apartment, distant from employment and Harlem. He subsequently noted tenseness, frequent masturbation, difficulty with his girlfriends, and then with his woman supervisor. He had lost that job before his analysis had begun.

During the historical recounting in the opening phase of treatment, the patient used Negro stereotypes to fend off the analyst. For example, he described how he had been asleep at the wheel during an accident in which a male friend had been killed and a girl injured. He sought to impress the analyst that his subsequent behavior toward the injured girl passenger involved minimal guilt and maximal underdependability. During this period of treatment, he also acted out by attempting intercourse with his step-mother's sister, related several incidents in which he presumably had gotten girls pregnant, and recounted several 'rape attempts.' He was finally able to recognize his desire to scare the analyst by exaggerating the material, 'You won't like me as much...do I want to be rejected and construct a situation?" At the same time, his directly verbalized anxieties about rejection related only to the building doormen and his feelings that he might be stopped on entering the lobby.

Dreams of the possibility, as well as the dangers, of a real concern for an attachment to a woman occurred shortly before he verbally recognized the analyst's pregnancy. Not only feelings of loss, but also those of considerateness, were mobilized for the first time. When the treatment resumed, he was attempting in vain to find his Spanish class, which he identified with passing. He felt that the analyst accepted the self-stereotyped rejected part of himself that he characterized as Negro. He later queried, 'I wonder if my coming to treatment would tend to make me feel equal to white?'

He became increasingly involved with color and in a dream indicated that Negro children and white women, including his mother, could be assertive because they had rights, while he as an adult Negro man, had none.[93]

One's sexuality and self-identity in the Black experience play a crucial role in the life of

Black individuals. In the case of the client above, "He associated only with men who were appreciably darker than himself," and he avoided fraternities that were "divided on color lines." The material uncovered through dream analysis revealed self-rejection due to blackness as realized in the client's search for his Spanish class, which he associated with "passing." This may only be a mirrored reflection of behavior manifested toward the fraternities, associating with darker men and holding the view that "coming to treatment would tend to make him feel equal to white."

The impact of racial stereotypes and myths upon transference and countertransference provides additional understanding on the dynamics of sex and race differences between worker and client. It is revealed in the case of **Mr. Y** above that white women as well as his mother, who was light complexioned, "could be assertive because they had rights, while he, as an adult **Negro** man, had none." The culminating experience of this scenario would place with the white male in complete authority of "assertiveness" and superiority, and the **Black male** being completely inferior and subordinate. This prevailing myth perpetuated in white American culture about "what white is" and "what Black isn't" is destructive to the Black/ white psyche and the entire dynamics of Black/ white relations. As one Black sociologist states:

> If you control a man's thinking, you do not have to worry about his action. When you determine what a man shall think, you do not have to concern yourself about what he will do. If you make a man feel that he is inferior, you do not have to compel him to accept an inferior status, for he will seek it himself. If you make a man think that he is just an outcast, you do not have to order him to the back door. He will go without being told; and if there is

> no back door, his very nature will de-
> mand one.[94]

The myths and stereotypes that have been created
over the centuries regarding Blacks and whites
are due in part to the lack of contact and associations between Blacks and whites and are partly
responsible for the lack of security in the
therapeutic relationship. Let us look at the
specific sexual stereotypes and myths regarding
the Black and white male and female sexual roles
and analyze the possible relevance of these
stereotypes to the transference and countertransference phenomena.

According to Cleaver, the sexual role definitions
and relationship of the Black/white society may
be divided as follows:

> **The Omnipotent Administrator** (white
> male)...possessing power and being the
> Thinker, wishing to preserve what they
> perceive as their superior position and
> way of life. 'Weakness, frailty,
> cowardice, and effeminacy are asso-
> ciated with the mind. Thus, the upper
> class, or Omnipotent Administrators,
> are perennially associated with physi-
> cal weakness, decay, underdeveloped
> bodies, effeminacy, sexual impotence
> and frigidity.' Cleaver explains that
> during the feudal society, the men of
> nobility, who were Omnipotent Adminis-
> trators by Divine Right, were con-
> sidered to have been weak, delicate,
> and effeminate.

> **The Super-Masculine Menial** (Black male)
> ...his attributes are just the opposite
> of the Omnipotent Administrator. Vir-
> ility, strength, and power are associ-
> ated with the Super-Masculine menial.
> He performs the 'Brute Power' function
> in society. His function is to carry
> out the assignment developed by the Ad-

120

ministrator. Of course, this is evident in every day life when one sees the Black male role in sports and the type of job assignments characteristic of the Black male. (The Heavyweight champion of the World, the Body man), the 'boy' mechanic, the 'boy' brick mason, **ad infinitum...**

The Ultra-Feminine Elite (white female)...the white male being the Omnipotent Administrator with the characteristics associated with it, is required to possess and project an image that is sharp contrast to his feminine counterpart. Therefore, the effeminate image of the male can still, by virtue of the sharp contrast in degree of femininity, be perceived as masculine. In other words, his woman must become Ultra-Feminine. In order to project the Ultra-Feminine image, she must abdicate the domestic function and take on the role of being tidy, neat, sweet and beautiful with all the frills. Her image is one of frailty, weakness, helplessness, delicacy, daintiness, silks, ruffles, etc.

The Subfeminine or Amazon (Black female)...she is deprived of her full womanhood by the fact that she has to take on the domestic functioning. She is characterized by dishpan hands, hard and rough.[95]

The above paradigm illustration by Cleaver is a direct correlation to many of the concerns inherent in the transference and countertransference dynamics of the Black worker and white client relationship.

As we look at the relationship between the white therapist and the Black client, we can see that the combination of Black sexuality and Black identity is pertinent to the whole question of stereotypes and how they may impinge on the therapeutic process between Black male and the white female. **Mr. Y.**, the Black male client of mixed racial blood in the case cited above, developed a transference attachment to the white female therapist based on the indoctrination and socialization he received from childhood through adulthood. As this case unfolds, we will see the dynamics of other factors related to the Super Masculine-Ultra Effeminine Elite paradigm.

The first possible indication of a positive transference in the relationship took place in the case of the unmarried Black man of mixed racial origin immediately following the client's recognition of the analyst's pregnancy. As we shall see, the client's development of a serious relationship with a female decreased his anxieties in therapy and created a positive transference reaction to therapist.

> He (client) insisted that he was basically ill-equipped for life, that the burdens of color and a poor cultural heritage increased his vulnerability, and that the analyst's attitude that he could make it only indicated how little she understood. At the same time, trust and mutuality developed through a discussion of The Invisible Man, which served as a vehicle for expression of his fears that the analyst would be paternalistic in setting his fee. For the first time he contemplated working in Harlem and enlarging upon the Negro stereotype.

> 'I've never worked around many colored people. I have stereotyped ideas of what the people would be like...more impulsive, physically impulsive, likely to hit out...I see whites as having more controls over themselves.'

Near the end of the second year of

122

analysis he began an affair with a blond white woman coworker, and during the analyst's second pregnancy he verbalized his feelings more meaningfully, and began to use insight to control himself. 'What kind of woman do I want...someone like you. I'm not going to get it while I'm doing all the talking.' The analyst demanded that he recognize and not give into his impulse to change all his relationships with women into sexual affairs, despite his increased awareness of anxiety and anger. He made an abortive attempt to escape into marriage, then returned to examine his feelings that he lacked the equipment to explore reality and his stereotypes. Months of angry resistence followed during which he repeatedly enunciated his desire to get what he wanted as a gift. Finally, however, he accepted the overtures of his white employer who became the first woman outside analysis with whom he had a friendly, non-sexual relationship. This brought color specifically back into the analysis, and after he invited her out to dinner he dreamed that he was castrated and had his penis in his hand.[96]

There is much material in this case illustration to be analyzed from the perspective of sexuality, self-identity and the Black psyche, including (1) the onset of the client's difficulty beginning with the client's move away from Harlem and the Black community, (2) self-hatred associated with being Black beginning at an early age with parents relocating because of his color, (3) identification with persons lighter than him, (4) stereotypical view of "other" Blacks as impulsive and view of white as reserved and controlled and many others. However, the apex of the transference transaction is demonstrated during the second year of analysis when the client "began an affair with a blonde white woman coworker." The ultimate question raised in his mind about the type of women he wanted was, "I want...someone like you," referring to the white female therapist.

Cleaver's paradigm on Black-white sexual roles and identifications has particular significance here given the client's negative and stereotypical attitude toward Black people and his positive mythical attitude toward white people. The white therapist and Black client are part of the same world where negative stereotypes depict Black sexuality and positive myths depict white sexuality. Therefore, the white therapist's response to the client who has been having difficulty establishing relationships with women is to warn the client "not give in to his (sexual) impulses by changing all his relationships with women into sexual affairs." In other words, do not let your **Super Masculine Menial** character dominate. The worker's attitude borders countertransference in that the traditional view of whites is to see Blacks as oversexed. First of all, there is no objective criteria to determine what is "over-doing it" in this particular case, and there is no clear-cut rational provided for suggesting that the client's behavior warrents control of his sexual "impulses."

Effective therapy during the course of four years resulted in the following:

> At the beginning of the fourth year of his analysis he met the young Negro professional woman he married two years later.[97]

Another case illustration involving the manifestation of sexual myths and stereotypes manifested in the white worker/Black client relationship may be seen in the case of **Mrs. Z.**

> Mrs. Z., a 25-year old, married, attractive, light-skinned Negro woman,

124

came for psychiatric help after experiencing an attack of panic. While
attending a fashion show, she began to
experience increasing anxiety and a
fear that she might scream. She left
the room, threw water on her face, and
soon felt relieved. Mrs. Z. recalled
two similar attacks in the previous
eighteen months.

One occurred while she was paticipating
in a casual discussion with her co-
workers; the second when having dinner
with her husband on a vacation trip.
In all three attacks, overwhelmed with
fear, she thought she would go insane
and yell out obscenities.[98]

The key factors that will be observed in this
case illustration are (1) the prevalence of unconscious significance of race, (2) the separation of presenting problems from racial concern,
(3) the need to address the issue of race with
the client even though it may not appear to be
relevant, (4) the inability of resolving the presenting problem when race is a concern without
first resolving the issue of race, (5) bringing
early childhood experiences with whites into present interaction with therapist and the added
dimension of (6) resolving the racial concern to
help alleviate the presenting problem even though
the presenting problem may appear to be separate.

From the beginning of the analysis,
Mrs. Z. was verbal, introspective, reported three to four dreams each week,
and presented a great deal of rich and
affect-laden material. For purposes of
this in the early months of the analysis, when news of marches and murders
were covering every paper's headlines
and pre-empting all other news on the
radio, the fact that a racial difference existed between patient and therapist never arose. References to these

daily occurrences or any feelings about
talking to a white man did not seem to
enter the patient's conscious mind. As
the months progressed, however,
Mrs. Z.'s dreams began to include more
and more references to color. In one
of her earliest dreams she went on a
trip with a friend and crossed the
D. C. line. She associated this to
running off and getting married in
Arlington, Virginia. In another dream,
she was purchasing light pink lipstick,
but the saleslady was getting ready to
close the shop, so she left without
making her purchase. In associating,
she said that pink had always been her
favorite color in clothing. In another
early dream, a tall dark man was walking on a winter night and the ground
was covered with white snow. There
were many other dreams and associations
to color and color differences.

Upon being confronted with this absence
of conscious thoughts about the racial
difference between patient and therapist despite the rather frequent references in her dreams to color, the patient began to express the concern she
had harbored since the beginning of the
analysis about the analyst being
Jewish. She assumed he was Jewish from
his name and appearance. She expressed
with considerable feelings her life-
long envy of Jewish people in her community. This was heavily tinged by a
general mistrust and resentment of
Jews.

With the following of further material,
this mistrust and dislike of Jews could
be understood, and had to be understood, on many levels. At the most superficial layer, the manifest content,
she had indeed been subjected to a

certain amount of racial discrimination and isolation in her white Jewish community. She recalled often feelings she could only go so far and no further with her school friends, and that she had been subtly excluded by her school-mates and treated condescendingly. She recalled a number of incidents of tra-veling in the South and having been barred from restaurants and movies be-cause of her color. Thus, starting treatment with someone who was white and Jewish stirred up many feelings and memories of her past which led to a sense of mistrust and discomfort.[99]

From the onset of therapy it is apparent that the worker was operating out of the view that "race is unimportant in the therapeutic relationship," and he failed to address the issue of race. How-ever, as the case progressed, we find that racial identify was important in the therapeutic rela-tionship. Secondly, when worker and client be-come conscious about racial differences, openness and ventilation occurred. Thirdly, the racial differences between worker and client had a cru-cial effect on the relationship given the client's stereotypes about Jews and her own per-sonal experiences with Jews. Therefore, the client brought to the therapeutic situation nega-tive feelings from prior experiences that were repressed and dormant until the discussion about racial differences was pursued. In fact, the client was verbal, introspective and engaged in the treatment process as though the differences in race were insignificant.

As the analysis proceeded, however, and her feelings about being Black and be-ing exposed to a white therapist were further explored and analyzed, the mul-tiple layers of unconscious meaning which found expression through the man-ifest interracial issue became appar-ent. For instance, it became clear that

unconsciously Mrs. Z's blackness came
to symbolize her instinctual drives and
fantasies. One of her earliest memories was playing in kindergarten, knowing that she was the only Negro in the
room, and feeling that she was different from everyone else. She remembered
the image she had of herself, influenced by the book 'Little Black Sambo'
as being dark black with kinky, oily
hair. In actuality she was only a few
shades darker than her playmates and
had straight brown hair. This memory,
which often came into her thoughts, she
associated to feelings of being different, bad, evil, and to her active mas-
turbatory activity at that time. She
reported a dream wherein some boys van-
dalized and viciously destroyed her
beige-colored car, and she chased after
them yelling, 'You Black bastards.'
She reported another dream in which a
black man came through her bedroom win-
dow. She felt terrified and helpless.
He pulled back her covers and was about
to rape her. Her thoughts about this
man led her to Stokely Carmichael and
how strikingly black he was when she
saw him on color television. In addition, she associated this to another
man who had recently made a pass at her
and she felt somewhat stimulated. It
was in connection with this dream that
she associated the previously mentioned
dream about wanting to buy pink lipstick, her favorite color.[100]

Again, the impact of the client's color and race
on the therapeutic relationship combined with
self-concept and sexuality of the client are constant variables in the white worker/Black client
relationship. The client above saw herself as
being "bad and evil" because of her blackness and
masturbation. There is a striking similarity

between this case and the case of **Mr. Y,** the unmarried Black male of mixed racial origin, where
the Black male associated his blackness with "the
reason his parents had to move" and the resultant
guilt of being Black. Furthermore, we see this
female client associating aberrant behavior with
blackness, such as "you Black bastards" vanda-
lized my car. At the same time there is a concomitant desire to escape blackness and become
"white" through an unconscious desire to be raped
by a Black man. The pink lipstick in the case of
Mrs. Z. is an attempt to identify with the white
female as the white Jewish analyst associated later in the analysis.

Let us observe the ultimate manifestation of
transference as the client attempted to act out
her sexual self-identity and concept with the
white male therapist:

> Interwoven with her struggle with her
> 'blackness,' Mrs. Z. utilized the
> therapist's whiteness and the concep-
> tional black-white racial barriers as
> the backdrop for her reawakened inces-
> tuous transference, wishes and con-
> flicts. At first there was an admira-
> tion of white men, and especially white
> doctors. She told countless stories
> about black-white couples and evidenced
> considerable envy of the girls who
> dated white men. A white friend was
> living with a militant Black man.
> Mrs. Z. could not understand how her
> friend was living with a militant Black
> man. Mrs. Z. could not understand how
> her friend could be attracted to this
> man, whom she felt to be gross and ugly
> because of his exaggerated Negroid fea-
> tures. Once Mrs. Z. went socially to a
> white psychiatrist's home and felt in
> awe of him. In association to this
> incident, she spoke of a Black psychia-
> trist she knew whom she felt was
> second-rate. She would not consider

seeing a Black doctor for medical care. Mrs. Z. gave birth to a child after the first year of analysis. Prior to delivery she was preoccupied with the fear that the baby would be dark and deformed. From her dreams and associations, this 'white' baby belonged to the analyst and came to be experienced as an extension of her own body.[101]

The transference reaction reaches a climax. There is the client's attraction for the white male therapist, which is sublimated through sexual interest in white men and envy of Black women with white men. In this case, as well as the case of, **Mr. Y,** the unmarried Black man of mixed racial origin, the white psychiatrists could have developed countertransference whereby they act out their fantasies through sexual involvement with the client. Yet, there are no case ilustrations available to suggest that this has ever been done. Nonetheless, the dynamics described in the cases above appear to be widespread in many case illustrations.

It is the effective handling of transference in the therapeutic process by the therapist that enables the client to overcome his/her difficulties. It is the self-awareness, racial awareness and sensitivity of the white therapist that will facilitate his/her role in walking the Black client through the transference experience with racial and sexual overtones.

The role of the white therapist with Black clients in addressing sexuality and self-concept may be the recognition and implementation of the following perspectives:

The white therapist should recognize the impact and relevance of sexual stereotypes and myths as they may complicate the worker/client relationship between different races and sexes.

The anti-Black hostilities and behavior of the white client toward the Black worker.[103]

The prohibition of self-disclosure by the white client with Black therapist due to guilt feelings of being an added burden to the already existing problems that the Black worker may face or the client's fear of being hurt and misunderstood by the Black worker.[104]

The white client's suspicion and distrust of the Black therapist's authority and competence due to the therapist's race[105] in contrast to the Black client's suspicion and distrust of the white therapist due to the possible racism of the white therapist and/or the view of the Black client that the white therapist is totally invested with competence because he/she is white.

The white client attributing negative qualities to the Black therapist[106] in contrast to the Black client attributing positive qualities to the white therapist.

The white client rejecting his/her sexual identity and self-concept associated with being white and attributing positive qualities to Black sexuality and the Black therapist.[107]

The white client's fear that the Black therapist will uncover unaware areas of racism[108] in contrast to the Black client's view that the white therapist is racist and incapable of understanding.

The white client's feeling of guilt for white society's treatment of Blacks[109] in contrast to the Black client's anger

at the way he/she is treated by white
society.

The white client who may internalize
the sexual myths and stereotypes regarding Blacks and transfer them to the
Black therapist[110] in contrast to the
Black client internalizing the sexual
myths about whites and projecting them
onto self.

The countertransference phenomenon involving the
Black therapist and white client relationship in
contrast to the white therapist and Black client
relationship shows:

The Black therapist attempting to prove
that he/she 'ain't Black' or 'anti-
white' and apologizing for his/her
Blackness to mitigate the guilt in the
white client in contrast to the white
therapist trying to prove that he/she
'ain't anti-Black' and apologizing for
his/her whiteness to alleviate the
Black client's anger and hostility.[111]

The conscious and/or unconscious anti-
white behavior of the Black
therapist[112] and the conscious and/or
unconscious anti-Black behavior of the
white client.

The view of the Black therapist that
working with white clients suggests a
high status[113] in contrast to the white
therapist's view that working with
Black clients is to advance a social
cause.

The need of the Black therapist to 'act
white' with white clients due to possibly unresolved feelings about his/her
own Blackness[114] in contrast to the
white therapist's need to deny identification with whites in order to

assuage his/her guilt.

The Black therapist adopting an ingratiating, 'Uncle Tom' attitude with a
white client in order to maintain his/
her client[115] in contrast to the con-
descending attitude of the white therapist with a Black client.

The Black therapist bringing to the
therapeutic relationship unresolved
feelings about Blackness[116] and uncon-
scious/conscious negative experiences
with whites in contrast to the white
therapists bringing unresolved con-
scious/unconscious, negative experiences with significant others in his/
her life regarding Blacks.

The Black therapist's view that he/she
will not be accepted by the white
client[117] in comparison to the white
therapist's view that he/she will not
be accepted by Black clients.

The willingness of both Black therapist
and the white therapist to deny the
significance of color and race in their
interaction with clients of the opposite race.[118]

The Black therapist being an unconscious symbol of the weak and negative
character of significant others in the
lives of the white client[119] in contrast to the white therapist taking on
the strong and negative characteristics
of significant others in the lives of
the Black client.

Relationship in Therapy

Much of what is illustrated above on the transference and countertransference dynamics of the

Black therapist with white client will be dramatized in the case illustration of **Miss K.** Let us
begin by looking at the strengths and weaknesses
of the more simple forms of transference and
countertransference in the Black worker/white
client relationship. The first and most general
reaction of the white client to the Black therapist is the anti-Black sentiment of the white
client. Let us observe the relationship and interaction of such a phenomenon in the case of
Miss K.

> Miss K. was an unmarried thirty-three-
> year-old white woman who had been diag-
> nosed as suffering from a schizophrenic
> reaction: chronic undifferentiated
> type. She was then on convalescent
> leave from a psychiatric hospital,
> having been released as greatly im-
> proved. Altogether she had been hospi-
> talized four times as a mental patient.
> On meeting the Negro worker in the ini-
> tial post-hospital interview, she ex-
> plicitly stated that she did not like
> his race, his looks, or his office.
> She said she would not return again and
> that the worker would have to drag her
> into the few evaluation interviews re-
> quired by the state. The worker ac-
> knowledged his concern and his sympathy
> for her feelings. He wondered if there
> might be some subject they could talk
> about, and he made some general comment
> about appreciating her frankness and
> honesty. His efforts failed to engage
> her at that point, but about three
> weeks later she telephoned and asked to
> see him. She said she was 'feeling
> funny' again and was thinking about
> suicide.
>
> She came into the interview promptly,
> and immediately said that she had been
> feeling very bad ever since she had
> said 'those nasty things' to the

worker. The worker pointed out that he did not recall her saying anything more than that she did not like Negroes, and he had appreciated her honesty. He reminded her that the function of the agency was to help her and that he had been appointed to see her for that purpose. Miss K., appearing to relax, said that she must have been thinking some 'funny things'; perhaps she had not said them after all; anyway, perhaps she should talk with the Negro worker, since she was always having 'dark thoughts.' The worker said that he did not know what the 'dark thoughts' were but that, if she wanted to help him understand they could arrange to see each other regularly. Miss K. accepted, commenting that maybe she would have something to live for then.[120]

There is an underlying social work premise that therapists should not view the response of a client (negative or positive) as a subjective reaction toward the therapist. This premise is supported by the dynamics of transference, which suggests that a client responds to the worker in the present as a significant other in his/her past. A major difficulty inherent in the Black therapist/white client relationship is that neither therapist nor client has escaped the scars of societal racism; furthermore, the relationship in therapy is not separate from the societal norms in which both patient and client live but is merely a reflection of culture. Yet, in spite of the many negative dynamics of race relations in contemporary American society, no consideration is given to the current relationship problems that may be existing between Blacks and whites in understanding transference. In the case of **Miss K.** it is demonstrated, however, that effective therapy can take place.

At first **Miss K.** vehemently rejected the Black

therapist and everything about him, including his physical make-up and his surroundings. The therapist's use of human sensitivity and human behavior acknowledged "concern and sympathy for the patient's feelings" even though those feelings were not favorable to the worker. Above all, the worker highlighted the strength in the client's "frankness and honesty" in exposing sensitive feelings about herself.

Effective use of therapy requires that the therapist works with the strengths of the client rather than the weaknesses. It is the role of the worker to identify the strengths. In the case of **Miss K.**, the Black therapist was able to identify the strengths of the client and look directly and honestly at the client's attitudes toward Negroes. The worker verbally acknowledged the client's reality without becoming insecure of his identity as a Black individual. There was an expression of accepting (acceptance) both the negative and the positive qualities of the client, which is essential to effective therapy. The therapist verbalized a willingness to join the client and help her through the difficulties she was experiencing with Blackness and Black people. The worker's expression that he could "appreciate her feelings" in spite of the fact that those feelings were directed toward him as the worker demonstrated strengths on the part of the worker.

Finally, the white client associated the psychological difficulties she was experiencing (those funny thoughts) with the negativeness of Blackness by identifying her experiences as "dark thoughts." The Black therapist expressed a willingness to try to understand and help the client through those feelings by scheduling regular appointments for the future. In this case, it is the client's negative association of "Blackness" with her "dark thoughts" that serves as a catalyst in the therapeutic relationship. The worker did not allow insecurities about racial identity to interfere with the therapeutic process.

Another case illustration dramatizing the dynamics of transference/countertransference in the
Black worker/white client relationship is the
case of a Black therapist and **Sonya,** an eleven-
year-old white girl. In this case a Black therapist denies his Blackness and the responses of
the client to him as a Black therapist. According to the worker:

> The patient, a rather bright, chubby
> eleven-year-old girl was first seen at
> the local mental health clinic at the
> age of six for excessive masturbation.
> The patient, referred to as Sonja, had
> been removed at the age of one year
> from her parents and placed by the wel-
> fare agency in a foster home where she
> was cared for by an elderly couple.
> She was adopted into her present home
> at the age of three years and five
> months.
>
> Within a few months after adoption,
> Sonja was seen to masturbate by the new
> parents, but they elected to ignore the
> problem until she began school. The
> disruption that her masturbatory habits
> had upon the class was apparently the
> key factor that led the parents to
> bring her to the mental health clinic.
>
> The parents had little contact with
> Blacks and were not aware that their
> child's therapist was Black until the
> mother and child came for their first
> appointment. The father had previously
> offered a great deal of resistance to
> participation, and had refused to ac-
> company his wife to therapy learning
> that his daughter would be working with
> a Black psychiatrist resident, he began
> to use race as an issue to support his
> continued uncooperativeness, stating

that he thought his daughter would develop racial attitudes that would be in conflict with those held by her community.

From the very first interview, her feelings regarding working with a Black psychiatrist were explored and she stated that 'race made no difference.' This was done purposefully to indicate to her that she was free to discuss race or racial issues as she liked. Our experience shows that early confrontation with racial issues tends to encourage the white client to express his feelings without fear, and to be comfortable in the knowledge that his Black therapist shares this freedom. The reader may feel that this approach may be merely reflecting paranoid feelings or defensiveness on the part of the Black therapist that he is, in fact, actually daring the patient to be prejudiced, or even that the approach is 'unanalytic.'

After approximately six months of treatment (on a once-a-week, 45 minutes basis) she decided to tell Dicken's Christmas Story about Scrooge as the ghost of the past, present, and future, and she metaphorically compared her life to that of the character Scrooge, who had seen the 'error of his ways' and was in need of change. Ironically enough, it was the Christmas season, and the patient brought the therapist as a present an antique which belonged to her father with his 'permission.' The act was interpreted as an indication of subtle changes in the father's attitude, and as his way of expressing appreciation for what he saw as improvement in his daughter. This 'permission' granted by the father had positive effects on the progress of therapy. Such a permission is most desirable, of course, under circumstances.[121]

The relevance of therapist addressing the issue of race in the casework relationship with clients continues to be of importance in race/ethnic differences of worker, but the client's attitude that "race makes no difference" proved to be erroneous and was, therefore, never fully addressed by the worker. The fact that the client identified with Scrooge in mending the "error of her ways" may have had relevance to her racial attitude and should have been explored by the therapist. The gift presented to the Black therapist by the client may have demonstrated her appreciation of her rectifying the "error of her ways." The fact that this was a special gift the client had received from her father, who disliked Black people, may have reinforced the thesis of mending the "errors of her ways," as well as attempts to mend the errors "of her father's ways." The dynamics involving this "special gift" may also suggest further unresolved racial matters affecting the client in that the client may have been attempting to dramatize the transfer of her love between father and therapist.

One of the key elements mentioned in the dynamics of transference and countertransference between therapist and client of different racial/ethnic groups is the impact that "significant others" play in the client's view of the worker. This is paramount in cases where the "significant others" may be present in the life of the client as with the 11-year-old because significant others may vicariously act out their frustrations and anxieties through the client. In the case of the ten-year-old who masturbated excessively, this did not appear to be a major problem. However, the therapist must be cognitive of such influences and the dynamics it may play in the therapeutic process. Just as the client may get conscious and/or unconscious clues as to how he/she should respond in a situation based on significant others, often, significant others present in the life of the client may consciously and/or unconsciously reward/punish the behavior of the client for vicarious gratification.

The more complex cases involving (1) self-identity, (2) sexuality, (3) self-concept, (4) the transmission of cultural stereotypes and (5) negative symbolism of Blackness as related to transference are to follow. The following case illustration provides some of the dynamics:

> A thirty-five-year old white professional man of Jewish extraction was referred by his cousin, a former patient of the analyst. He sought analysis because of his inability to get married. During each of two engagements, he had become progressively depressed and anxious and in each instance had broken off the relationship. A second complaint, premature ejaculation, had begun a year before the patient sought help. Vocationally, he was insecure despite the fact that he worked in an executive capacity. He was ingratiating with fellow employees and fearful that he might not be able to control his anger in work situations.

> His most vivid memories of early childhood dated back to age six, with recollections of visits to his white Jewish aunt and grandmother in Harlem. He took pride in making the subway trips alone, but recalled mixed feelings of anxiety and excitement. The Harlem community of that period was racially integrated. His anxiety was predicated upon his fear of physical attack, and his excitement seemed rooted in sexual fantasies which utilized racial stereotypes and myths.[122]

At first, we see the transmission of cultural (sexual) stereotypes regarding Blacks emanating at an early age on the client's visit to Harlem, as reported by the therapist. As the case illustration progresses, we will see the significant aspect that this "excitement/anxiety" ambivalence plays in the difficulties experienced by this client as well as its impact on transference with the Black therapist. The age-old racial myths and stereotypes about Black sexual superiority and dominance and the white sexual inferiority and submissiveness are played out here. The only unique difference in this scenario is the white male internalizing these stereotypes and their impact on his sexual self-identity and concept. The client's "fantasy of excitement" and anticipated "joys and pleasures of the forbidden" coupled with anxieties and insecurities about being white became the impetus for the presenting problem.

The client's sexual dilemma was complicated by his view that being white would make him more worthy of a sexual attack by Black males in that the Black male stereotypically regards the white male as effeminate and weak. In this instance, however, the white male created a delusion in his mind based on the stereotype that he is or should be the target of the Black male impulsive sexual agressiveness. The dynamics of this sexual agressiveness. The dynamics of this delusion may be peculiar to the ingredients of the "pathology" in the client's family interaction as indicated in the psychosocial history.

> An intense fear of losing his parents prevaded his childhood. He was a good student and active in athletics, but frequently needed his mother's intervention on his behalf during altercations with other children. At home, his mother was a severely critical, domineering, anxious woman who subjugated her husband and chided him for being weak, inadequate, and a poor

142

provider. She lamented her difficult
lot in life and confided the intimacies
of her marital dissatisfaction to the
patient. The father was physically and
emotionally inaccessible.

Castration anxiety increased at age
fourteen when his parents' concern
about the size of his penis led them to
consult a physician. He was embar-
rassed to shower with schoolmates for
fear that they would discover that his
penis was small. Adolescence brought
sexual interest and exploration; he
dated, but was always inhibited and
anxious.

Concern about the size of his penis
persisted into adulthood. After com-
pletion of Army service and college, he
worked in an executive position, continuing to live with his parents. He
perceived phallic women as castrators,
and used prematurity and impotence to
defend against castration. With men,
he was 'the nice guy,' obsequious, ingratiating, and controlling his rage.
His nonassertiveness socially, sexually, and vocationally was a derivative
of his need to control his rage.

Early dreams gave form to the negative
transference of the first six months
and highlighted one of the patient's
key problems: the Negro man was presented as physically assaultive, drunk,
and debased, and the patient feared his
analyst's aggression and sexual exploitation.

In his associations he dwelt on the
theme of the menacing Negro, juxta-
posing his sexual inadequacy, fear of
women, and his perception of women as
castrating, humilating creatures. Soon

143

after beginning the analysis he moved
from his parents' home, magically utilizing the therapist's strength as a
buffer against his mother. The move
was accompanied by a great deal of
anxiety, represented in dreams as a
fear of starving to death. He began to
date and to attempt sex, expressing his
lack of assertiveness and his dependency orientation in dreams...[123]

The transference reaction reaches a symbolic
climax. In the dream analysis, "the Negro man
was presented as physically assaultive, drunk and
debase, and the patient feared his analyst's aggression and sexual exploitation." It is apparent that the repressed anger of the client
along with ingratiation with fellow employees,
insecurity about sexual identity and inability to
establish a relationship with females may be
attributed to maternal overdominance. To a large
extent, the Black therapist was identified as the
strong and domineering "mother" with the ac-
companying cultural stereotypes. Needless to
say, the impact of internal family dynamics and
the cultural stereotypes may be different and
separate but part and particle of the same
dynamics. The therapist elaborated sufficiently
on the emphasis of the size of the client's penis
and its relationship to therapy. However, the
client's view of women as castrators and his insecurity about his own sexual identity dramati-
cized by an over concern about his penis size may
be looked at as a reaction to a dominant mother.
Finally, the apparent threat presented by the
Black therapist seemed to have involved all the
factors of mother dominance, concern for penis
size and transmission of cultural stereotypes.

Ten months after the beginning of
analysis he triumphantly reported that
he was able to penetrate a women
sexually despite intense anxiety and
fear of impregnating her. He plied the
analyst with questions about contracep-

tion, in actuality seeking plaudits for his sexual accomplishments. The analyst's mild disbelief in the therapeutic significance of the patient's achievement in part reinforced the patient's stereotyped perception of the Negro as a virile sexual superman, thus widening the gulf between analyst and client. Another source of difficulty during this period was the analyst's need to disclaim his therapeutic power to achieve such a great effect with the patient. This problem was rooted in the analyst's insecurity about his effectiveness which was combined, however, with a need to assert his greater power over the patient.[124]

The white male client appears to have provoked a countertransference transaction given the Black therapist's reactions to the client's sexual exploits. The fact of the matter is that it is a cultural practice in the Black society for young, Black males to "brag about their sexual exploits" and the size of their penis to justify their manhood. To a greater or lesser degree, the same is true of all American cultures. Nonetheless, the making of a countertransference developed.

Given the above countertransference reaction, however, the obvious occurred. The client retreated in self-disclosure and progress is impeded; therefore, the client found further justificaions for remaining ill, as in earlier experiences with significant others and in resolving issues of self-identity and concept. The author continues:

> With continued attempts at intercourse, a pseudohomosexual theme emerged in a dream.
>
> I was in bed with S. She got on top of me. We were having intercourse. But it was not S's face. It was a Man's

face. I was frightened.

He discussed the anxiety in the dream, adding 'I'm afraid of women so a man is safer. But why am I afraid of women? My mother is a woman.'

The second year of analysis was concerned with his efforts to separate emotionally from his parents, to improve his sexual adaptation, and to deal with his chronic anxiety. During this period he maintained a relationship with one woman, advanced vocationally, and began to see himself as having an existence separate from that of his parents, with lessening anxiety about their death. Reference to the therapist's race was minimal, although when the patient's fear of the therapist mounted, the menacing Negro would reappear in his dream life.

A Negro trooper strikes a white policeman in the stomach. The white man beats him up.[125]

The above dynamics merely dramatized the intensity of the sexual conflict experienced by the white client and stimulated by family dynamics, cultural stereotypes and the therapist's race. The "conclusion" of the therapeutic interaction adds, clarifies and further illustrates the depth of the transference and countertransference dynamics. The worker concludes:

Increased separation from his family brought mounting anxiety about his relationship with the analyst, and he reconsidered his childhood visits to his aunt's home in Harlem, which were marked by a mixture of pleasurable excitement and fear. The omission of his father's role in the family, previously justified by his father's absence at

146

work during the patient's childhood, became a therapeutic focus, particularly since any information about the father had been transmitted by the mother. During the latter part of the second year of analysis, material emerged indicating that his father had protected him against the mother and against destructive women in general. His dreams became less frighteningly destructive and he dreamed of father and therapist in terms of helping figures. He was married in the third year of analysis and terminated six months later. His functioning had improved considerably in all areas.[126]

Here we move to even more significant transference data in terms of the client's reassessment of his father's role as "protector of him from a domineering mother" rather than being weak, submissive and isolated. This new insight, again was reenacted into the dreams of "father and therapist in terms of helping figures." It was the revelation of this new perspective reenacted with the therapist that may have been the focal point of successful treatment for the patient; but at the same time, this revelation may have proven to be most detrimental. Further interactions between worker and client illustrated the unconscious desire on the part of the client to realize and actualize the transference phenomena. The author concludes:

In fact, he concretized this wish by introducing himself to the analyst in the men's room of a banquet hall at the time of his cousin's wedding.[127]

As demonstrated in many cases of the white worker and Black client relationship, the client's desire to actualize the symbolic transference experience may be acted out in other areas of the client's life. The therapist's realization of this process enables the worker to help the client confront those realities and reach a resolution to the problem.

In the same manner that there are factors that the white therapist must consider in his/her relationship with Black clients, there are factors that the Black therapist must consider in his/her relationships with the white client. These include self-awareness, self-insight, growth and proper utilization of therapeutic skills. The variables of race, self-disclosure and sexual stereotypes should be analyzed in the Black worker/white client realtionship. Some of the factors to be considered in the Black worker/white client relationship are as follows:

Exploration of the meaning of racial differences between therapist and client early in the therapeutic process whether it appears to be relevant or not.

Worker's openness and willingness for continuous growth in self-awareness and self-insight.

Openness and willingness of the worker to take a risk by exposing anxieties about being Black through exploring pertinent content with white client.

Willingness of the worker to grow and learn from mistakes made and insight revealed through clients.

Worker's recognition of countertransference and quickness to make adjustment in therapy.

Worker's exploration of over-identification, ingratiation and anti-white attitudes in search of self-awareness.

The Black therapist's acceptance of the

white client as a unique individual rather than as a mere reflection or stereotype of the "white race."

The therapist's recognition that he/she is not "resolving the problems of racism and race relations by helping a white client"; rather, the therapist is only helping one individual.

The Black therapist's clear exploration and analysis of his/her psyche needs in working with white clients in spite of the fact that the therapeutic relationship may be involuntary.

The Black therapist's familiarity with the dynamics of white supremacy on the psyche of whites in order to determine the overt and convert adaptive mechanism of whites to Blacks as its implication for the worker/client interaction.

The Black therapist's familiarity with the dynamics of white supremacy/Black oppression on the psyche of Blacks to assess the overt and convert adaptive mechanism of Blacks to whites as it may pertain to his/her interaction with a white client.

The Black therapist's recognition that he/she is not totally free of prejudice and should not respond to a position where he/she is being asked to "prove that you are not prejudiced: and/or prove your equality.

The therapist's ability to do away with the obvious racist stereotypes that automatically associate Black people with everything negative and white people with everything positive.

The following case provides an added dimension

that relates to the fear of white clients that the Black therapist may blame the white client for the atrocities perpetuated against the Black race. Secondly, there is the corresponding fear that the Black therapist is going to use the therapeutic process to "get back" at the white client. According to the worker:

> A 34-year-old Jewish man who came to treatment because of severe and incapacitating phobias also had great difficulty in handling his money. He seemed to have a compulsive need to squander his more than ample earnings. He made an elaborate show of his lack of racial prejudice. At the time of referral he was not told that I was Negro and seemed delighted at this opportunity to demonstrate his lack of ill-will toward Negroes. He found it impossible to identify with me as a member of a minority and thought of himself as a spy in the Anglo-Saxon Protestant world of big business. It was, however, in the world of money that he found it necessary to use our racial difference for a defensive purpose.
>
> As time went on, it became clear that he seemed askew of his high income and most reluctant to allow me to know exactly how much he made. By analysis of dreams and fantasies it was made clear that he identified himself with Jewish businessmen whom he felt had exploited Negroes in the past. On one occasion he described Jewish wealth as tainted because it was stolen from hard working, native Negroes. Inasmuch as he was Jewish, earning a large salary, and felt himself to be at the mercy of a Negro whom he imagined to be better trained but earning less than he -- he was terrified. He imagined that I

would punish him for all the wrongs he imagined Jews had vested on Negroes.

His resistance was rooted in the conviction that I had personally been victimized by Jews and therefore had to feel the personal resentment he feared. He viewed this as a realistic impasse which prevented our dealing with his neurosis. It was resolved only after I granted that there must have been a time when I was exploited by Jews and no doubt resented it.

But the same could be said for my contacts with Americans, Poles, Swedes, and many other ethnic groups -- did he really think that I was nursing long past grievances toward all those groups? And WASPS -- did he really think that it was impossible for me to deal reasonably with reasonable whites? If so, then it would clearly be impossible for me to function amiably with Negroes since, living with them, I would naturally have been hurt more by them. Was it not more likely that he attributed something more vicious, more hostile to Jewish exploitation of Negroes and were we not back on the familiar ground of his projecting his own (hostile) feelings onto a large global (and in this case ethnic) screen?[128]

In the same manner that it is not an easy task for the white therapist to avoid feeling guilty about the pains inflicted by white society onto the Black client, it is no easy task for the Black therapist to avoid punitiveness toward white clients. The best that can be accomplished is for the therapist, in both instances, to be willing to share openly, honestly and reciprocally in his/her relationship for direction and resolution to the factors of race in the

151

relationships. It is the responsibility, however, of the therapist to lead the way, utilizing
the skills of self-awareness and the openness to
learn something about self as the guide.

In the case of the thirty-four-year old Jewish
man, however, the Black therapist demonstrated
competence in his reactions to the client's fear
of being hurt in therapy. First of all, the
Black therapist acknowledged that he may have
been exploited by the Jews "at one time" due to
his Blackness and that he no doubt resented it."
The Black therapist addressed the concern directly and openly to those statements. Nonetheless, for many Blacks the personal feelings of
resentment from exploitation may not be as remote
as "something in the past." Those feelings may
be in the present "here and now." Even so, the
worker's recognition and verbalization of those
facts may serve a therapeutic purpose. By the
Black therapist reassuring the white client that
he/she is not going to let the factors of race
"get into the way" of the therapeutic process,
the foundation for effective therapy is built.
In fact, it may be helpful for the Black therapist to ask the client to bring it to the attention of the worker when there is a feeling that
the worker is responding negatively due to race.

A worker should always have a sensitive response
to a client's concern about being a scapegoat in
therapy due to racial differences between worker
and client. For example, a white therapist's use
of rationalization, theoretical propositions and
didactic responses such as "other minority groups
made it, so can you" will be ineffective. This
kind of attitude and response may be good in
theory (although we know this is not true), but
it does not tell the client how the therapist
feels about him/her on an affective level. A
Black therapist's response to a white client that
"I am not the problem...you are the problem" will
also be ineffective.

Another case illustration involving a forty-year-

old white executive with a Black male therapist
will magnify and illustrate other components of
the Black worker/white client relationship.

> A forty-year-old white executive en-
> tered treatment because of anxiety and
> work inhibition. He immediately dis-
> missed the idea that he felt any racial
> prejudice and said that on that account
> our racial differences need not come
> up. Surprisingly, for months his ap-
> praisal seemed accurate and there was
> nothing in the material to suggest that
> I was even perceived as a Negro.
>
> In time a theme of jealous and inten-
> sive rivalry toward his brother
> emerged. He had been the youngest of
> three sons and had always felt left out
> of the grown-up doings of his father
> and brothers. He was indulged by his
> mother, and developed a feeling of rel-
> ative effeminancy, although overt homo-
> sexuality never posed a problem.
>
> As this theme was elaborated his atti-
> tude toward me took on a cold, suspi-
> cious tone. How could he be sure I
> truly meant to help him? Was I not
> really jealous of him and his business
> successes? How could he be sure I was
> not secretly undermining his confi-
> dence, weakening his capacity, so that
> he would fail in his job? Then, fi-
> nally, after all, he was white, and I
> could not possibly feel the compassion
> and involvement toward him that I felt
> toward my Negro patient.[129]

The aspect of this case that is basically different and unique from the other cases relates to
the transfer of negative qualities of significant
others onto the Black therapist. This may be
disguised when the issue of race may appear ir-
relevant in the therapeutic transference process.

The therapist "taking on the negative characteristics" of the significant others in the life
of the client may not be entirely unique to racial differences in worker and client. For that
very reason, it is possible that the Black male
therapist preferred to focus on the white
client's jealousy of other Black clients rather
than the relationship existing between the two of
them.

> He managed to isolate the jealousy of
> his brothers form his jealousy of my
> Negro patients in an impassioned, and
> at times, paranoid manner. He was able
> to feel the intensity of his rivalry
> with other patients while his feelings
> toward his brothers remained sterile,
> two-dimensional recollections.[130]

Finally, we will look at a case involving a Black
male therapist and white female patient and the
peculiar dynamics of transference as pertaining
to sexuality and self-identity:

> A 32-year-old white Anglo-Saxon woman
> of Southern U. S. origin entered treat-
> ment because of progressively incapaci-
> tating anxiety. Initially, she ignored
> the subject of race since her anxiety
> was of such paramount importance, but
> with an amelioration of her presenting
> symptoms, her dreams and fantasies in-
> dicated that the matter of race had to
> be considered. She admitted reluc-
> tantly some feelings of shame that her
> psychiatrist was a Negro. She could
> never tell her friends for fear of what
> they might think. Indeed, it finally
> came out that she had never told her
> husband that I was a Negro. Simul-
> taneously, material began to appear
> which clearly indicated that the trans-
> ference had assumed an erotic quality.

The denouncement was as follows: She

had erected the fantasy that I found her sexually irresistible, and since she had heard that Negroes had little impulse control, she expected each session to have her sexual desires gratified. I was her (potentially) secret lover, eminently accomplished in matters of this kind and one with whom she could for the first time let herself go. She was unconsciously experiencing a tumultuous affair with a dark secret lover and all under the guise of respectable psychotherapy.[131]

The impact of understanding the sexual dynamics in the Black male therapist and white female client and white female therapist and the Black male client relationship must be looked at in relationship to the myths regarding sexual stereotypes. It is the nature of these stereotypes and symbols that provides the basis for dissecting the difficulties involved.

Needless to say, the stage is set in the case of this young, thirty-two-year old white female, in therapy with this Black male worker. As generic to most of the cases discussed, the issue of race did not appear to be a problem at first. However, as the case develops, we find the client attempting to actualize the cultural stereotypes through her delusions that she, being white, is "irresistable to the Black male"; furthermore, the sexual attachment of the white female to the therapist demonstrates an assimilation of the sexual cultural stereotypes prevelant in the society. In addition, it is apparent that the role played by "significant others" in the life of the white female client may impede the therapeutic process as well. The catalytic effect of such dynamics in this case is clearly defined when the following occurred:

In fact her husband, when told, thought the matter of my race of little moment; the Oedipal conflicts she had sought to

act out with me could then be uncovered
and treatment could progress without
further significant racial impediment.[132]

In conclusion, the following factors must be
recognized by the Black therapist when working
with white clients:

The Black therapist should recognize
that he/she has "power" and "authority"
in the worker/client relationship and
need not prove it.

The Black therapist should recognize
that he/she is qualified for the position and need not have to "prove it."

The Black therapist should understand
the dynamics of sexual stereotypes and
how they may interfere in the trans-
ference/countertransference phenomenon.

The Black therapist must understand the
significance that the symbol of color
and race may play in the transference
and countertransference phenomenon.

The Black therapist must understand the
significance of being a member of a
race associated with inferiority and
the impact of this on transference and
countertransference.

The Black therapist must not adopt the
notion the "I understand you better
than you understand you because I am
Black." The Black therpaist must be
willing to listen and learn.

The Black therapist should not be
threatened by negative transference
when the client may be hostile but
recognize the strength in the ability
of the client to express such feelings.

The Black therapist shoud not be misled by positive transference as being an indication that the issue of race may not be a concern in therapy.

81. Lois Pettit. "Some Observation on Negro Culture in the United States," Social Work, Vol. 5, No. 3, (July, 1960).

82. Shirley Cooper. "A Look at the Effect of Racism on Clinical Work," Social Casework, Vol. 54, (February, 1973).

83. Jean S. Gochros. "Recognition and Use of Anger in Negro Clients," Social Work, Vol. II, No. 1, (January, 1966), pp. 29-30.

84. Judith S. Schachter and Hugh F. Butts. "Transference and Countertransference in Interracial Analysis," Journal of the American Psychoanalytic Association, Vol. 16, No. 4, (October, 1968), pp. 800-801.

85. Barbara B. Solomon. Black Empowerment: Social Work in Oppressed Communities, (New York: Columbia University Press, 1976), pp. 311-312.

86. Alex Gitterman and Alice Schaeffer. "The White Professional and the Black Client," Social Casework, Vol. 53, (May, 1972), pp. 280-291.

87. Shirley Cooper. "A Look at the Effect of Racism on Clinical Work," Social Casework, (February, 1973).

88. Ibid. p. 79.

89. Langston Hughes. The Panther and the Lash, (New York: Alfred A. Knopf, 1969), p. 85.

90. Esther Fibush. "The White worker and the Negro Client," Social Casework, Vol. XLVI, (May, 1965), p. 275.

91. Ronald G. Lewis and Man Keung Ho. "Social Work with Native Americans," Social Work, (September, 1975).

William Grier and Price M. Cobbs. <u>Black Rage</u>, (New York: Bantam Books. 1968).

Julia Bloch. "The White Worker and the Negro Client in Psychotherapy," <u>Social Work</u>, Vol. 13, No. 2, (April, 1968).

Mayard Calnek. "Racial Factors in the Countertransference: The Black Therapist and the Black Client," <u>American Journal of Orthopsychiatry</u>, Vol. 40, No. 1, (January, 1970).

92. Judith S. Schachter and Hugh F. Butts. "Transference and Countertransference in Interracial Analysis," <u>Journal of the American Psychoanalytic Association</u>, Vol. 16, No. 4, (October, 1968), p. 798.

93. Ibid. p. 799.

94. Carter G. Woodson. <u>The Miseducation of the Negro</u>, (New York: AMS Press, 1972). Introduction XIII.

95. Eldridge Cleaver. <u>Soul on Ice</u>, (New York: McGraw-Hill Book Company, 1968), pp. 164-190.

96. Judith S. Schachter and Hugh F. Butts. "Transference and Countertransference in Interracial Analysis," <u>Journal of The American Psychoanalytic Association</u>, Vol. 16, No. 2, (October, 1968), p. 799.

97. Ibid. p. 800.

98. Newell Fischer. "An Interracial Analysis: Transference and Countertransference Significance," <u>Journal of the American Psychoanalytic Association</u>, Vol. 19, No. 4, (1971), pp. 736-745.

99. Ibid. pp. 736-745.

100. Ibid. pp. 736-745.

101. Ibid. pp. 736-745.

102. LaMaurice H. Gardner. "Psychotherapy Under
     Varying Conditions of Race" in Roderick W.
     Pugh (ed.) Psychology and the Black
     Experience (Belmont: Brooks/Cole
     Publishing Company; a division of Wadsworth
     Publishing Company, Inc. 1972).

103. Andrew Curry. "The Negro Worker and the
     White Client" A Commentary on the Treatment
     Relationship," Social Casework, Vol. XIV.
     No. 3. (1964).

104. Ibid.

105. LaMaurice H. Gardner. "Psychotherapy Under
     Varying Conditions of Race" in Roderick W.
     Pugh (ed.) Psychology and the Black
     Experience (Belmont: Brooks/Cole Publishing
     Company; a division of Wadsworth Publishing
     Company, Inc. 1972).

106. J. Hamilton. "Some Dynamics of Anti-Negro
     Prejudices," Psychoanalytic Review,
     Vol. 53: "Psychological Factors in Negro
     Race Hatred and in Anti-Negro Riots,"
     Vol. 32, (1962), and T. C. Rodgers, "The
     Evaluation of an Active Anti-Negro Racist,"
     in W. Muensterberger and S. Axelrod (eds.),
     The Psychoanalytic Study of Society, Vol. 1,
     (New York: International Universities.
     1960).

107. LaMaurice H. Gardner. "Psychology Under
     Varying Conditions of Race" in Roderick W.
     Pugh (ed.) Psychology and The Black
     Experience, (Belmont: Brooks/Cole
     Publishing Company, 1972). Also see:
     William H. Grier, "When the Therapist is
     Negro: Some Effects on the Treatment
     Process," American Journal of Psychiatry,
     Vol. 123, No. 12, (June, 1967) and Judith S.

Schachter and Hugh F. Butts, "Transference and Countertransference in Interracial Analysis" <u>Journal of the American Psychoanalytic Association</u>, Vol. 16, No. 6, (October, 1968).

108. LaMaurice H. Gardner. "Psychology Under Varying Conditions of Race" <u>in</u> Roderick W. Pugh (ed.) <u>Psychology and the Black Experience</u>, (Belmont: Brooks/Cole Publishing Company, 1972).

109. William Grier. "When the Therapist is Negro: Some Effects on the Treatment Process," <u>American Journal of Psychiatry</u>, Vol. 123, No. 12, (June, 1967).

110. Judith S. Schachter and Hugh F. Butts. "Transference and Countertransference in Interracial Analysis," <u>Journal of American Psychoanalytic Association</u>, Vol. 16, No. 4, (October, 1968). <u>See also</u>: William Grier, "When the Therapist is Negro: Some Effects on the Treatment Process," <u>American Journal of Psychiatry</u>, Vol. 123, No. 12, (June, 1967).

111. LaMaurice H. Gardner. "Psychology Under Varying Conditions of Race" <u>in</u> Roderick W. Pugh (ed.) <u>Psychology and the Black Experience</u>, (Belmont: Brooks/Cole Publishing Co., 1972).

112. Leonard C. Simmons. "'Crow Jim': Implications for Social Work," <u>Social Work</u>, (July, 1963).

113. LaMaurice H. Gardner. "Psychology Under Varying Conditions of Race," op. cit.

114. Ibid.

115. Ibid.

116. Ibid.

117. Ibid.

118. Ibid.

119. William Grier. "When the Therapist is
      Negro: Some Effects on the Treatment
      Process," American Journal of Psychiatry,
      Vol. 123, No. 12, (June, 1967). See also:
      Judith Schachter and Hugh F. Butts,
      "Transference and Countertransference in
      Inter-Racial Analysis," Journal of the
      American Psychoanalytic Association,
      Vol. 16, No. 4, (October, 1968).

120. Andrew E. Curry. "The Negro Worker and the
      White Client: A Commentary on the Treatment
      Relationship," Social Casework, Vol. VLV,
      No. 3, (March, 1964), p. 132.

121. James H. Carter and Thomas M. Haizlip.
      "Race and Its Relevance to Transference,"
      American Journal of Orthopsychiatry,
      Vol. 42, (October, 1972), p. 173-175.

122. Judith S. Schachter and Hugh F. Butts.
      "Transference and Countertransference in
      Inter-Racial Analysis," Journal of the
      American Psychoanalytic Association,
      Vol. 16, No. 4, (October, 1968), p. 795.

123. Ibid. p. 796.

124. Ibid. p. 797.

125. Ibid. p. 797

126. Ibid. p. 798

127. Ibid. p. 802.

128. William Grier, "When the Therapist is Negro:
      Some Effects on the Treatment Process,"
      American Journal of Psychiatry, Vol. 123,
      No. 12, (June, 1967), p. 1588.

129. Ibid. pp. 1589-1590.

130. Ibid. p. 1590.

131. Ibid. p. 1589.

132. Ibid. p. 1589.

Chapter IV

SOCIAL CASEWORK INTERVENTION: NATIVE
AMERICANS, PUERTO RICANS, MEXICAN AMERICANS
AND SELECTED ORIENTAL AMERICANS

NATIVE AMERICAN

The factor of cultural conflicts appears to be
the major inhibiting element between a worker and
a client of Native American origin as opposed to
the factors of racial hostilities, anger and conflict that exist within the Black/white, client/
worker relationships. Given the literature available on Puerto Ricans, Mexican Americans and Native Americans in social casework, the major focus appears to be on the cultural interaction
taking place between worker and client rather
than on the impact of racism. Yet, in the same
way that there are misunderstandings, negative
stereotypes and racism confronting Blacks, the
same is true of the Native American. There is a
feeling by Native Americans that there are no
other people more misunderstood as the American
Indians. They are also plagued wih myths regarding their way of life, thinking, customs and attitudes. There is the view that these myths have
influenced the ideas of Indian and non-Indian
alike in the same manner that the myths and
stereotypes regarding Blacks and other minorities
have influenced both the majority as well as the
minority culture. For those social workers, anthropologists and social scientists who have observed the Native American culture, there is
agreement on the following commonalities existing
in the Native American cultures:

> The mass media, via television, is re-
> sponsible for perpetuating many of the
> negative stereotypical views of Native
> Americans.[133]

In Native American culture there is the

inherent value of **sharing** with
others.[134]

Native Americans have a circular concept of time based on the moon, sun and
seasons as opposed to the linear concept existing in the Western culture,
which is composed of dividing time into
minutes, seconds, hours, days, weeks,
months, and years.[135]

The Indians view self as an integral
part of nature working and living in
harmony with nature as opposed to being
separate from nature, which is inherent
in the Western world view. Therefore,
Native Americans do not 'kill animals
for sport,' 'pollute the water for
technological advancement.' (They never took more from nature than they
could consume.)[136]

There is intrinsic respect and value
for the elderly as extended family.[137]

The Native American extended family
value system includes living arrangements and psychological as well as physical support.[138]

There is an intrinsic value of **coopera-
tion** with others rather than **comp-
etitiveness.**[139]

Family needs are **first** priority.[140]

There is a circular concept of space
and time in viewing the past, present
and future as all part of a whole rather than evaluating time and space as
progressive and linear.

There is a **strong** belief in the influence of a Supreme Being having an im-

pact on life rather than the cause-effect explanation of behavior per-petuated in the Western society.[142]

Native Americans view **good** and **bad** as being part of a whole rather than sepa-rate entities. Therefore, there is the notion of acceptance of the ill effects of life as natural and expected, and these should be included in the same manner as the joys of life.[143]

Native Americans emphasize the impor-tance of human relations and harmony over materialism and technological ad-vancement when the two may be in con-flict.[144]

The relevance of the cultural variables described above can be demonstrated in the following exam-ple of casework intervention with a Native American client. This case illustration of the Redthunder family will amplify a few of the major points regarding the uniqueness of the Native American culture and the implication for social casework intervention.

The Redthunder family was brought to the school social worker's attention when teachers reported that both child-ren had been tardy and absent frequent-ly in the past weeks. Since the worker lived near Mrs. Redthunder's neighbor-hood, she volunteered to transport the children back and forth to school. Through this regular but informal ar-rangement, the worker became acquainted with the entire family, especially with Mrs. Redthunder who expressed her gra-titude to the worker by sharing her home-grown vegetables.[145]

At the onset, we can see that the worker's knowl-ledge of the client's culture is a major facili-tative factor. The social caseworker suggests that it is the custom of the Native American to talk periphally about unimportant matters before confronting the core of his/her present problem. The potential for difficulties to develop between worker and client in a situation similar to this one is intensified due to the possible **impatience** of the trained therapist to view his/her responsibility as remaining **formal** and **directed** rather than spending time "getting acquainted" with the client. However, a worker's lack of awareness of the Native American unique cultures coupled with inadequate professional skills would always be a major obstacle to effective social work intervention.

As the **informal stage** between Mrs. Redthunder and the worker is developed, a significant aspect of this casework relationship unfolds. We can see the Native American traditional value of sharing as the establishment of rapport and communication develops. Furthermore, we can see the impact that this knowledge has on the therapeutic relationship. The case continues:

> The worker sensed that there was much family discomfort and that a tumultuous relationship existed between Mr. and Mrs. Redthunder. Instead of probing into their personal and marital affairs, the worker let Mrs. Redthunder know that she was willing to listen should the woman need someone to talk to. After a few gifts of home-grown vegetables and Native American handicrafts, Mrs. Redthunder broke into tears one day and told the worker about her husbnad's problem of alcoholism and their deteriorating marital relationship.[146]

The most important element in this therapeutic process is that the therapist utilized the Native American's cultural tradition of "keeping things in the family" and the principle of non-interference in social work intervention. The therapist made the client cognizant of her empathy, concern and availability to help rather than probe and violate the Native American's cultural values. The manifestation of the Native American's cultural value of **sharing** is again noted, and we can see a breakthrough in the case. In conclusion, we come to the ultimate transaction of the worker's acceptance of the Native American cultural realities:

> Realizing Mr. Redthunder's position of respect in the family and his resistance to outside interference, the social worker advised Mrs. Redthunder to take her family to visit the minister, a man whom Mr. Redthunder admired. The Littleaxe family, who were mutual friends of the worker and the Redthunder family, agreed to take the initiative in visiting the Redthunders more often. Through such frequent but informal family visits, Mr. Redthunder finally obtained a job, with the recommendation of Mr. Littleaxe, as recordkeeper in a storeroom. Mr. Redthunder enjoyed his work so much that he drank less and spent more time with his family.[147]

It is impossible to evaluate the element of transference and countertransference in the **Redthunder** case because the cultural dynamics of **noninterference** is diametrically opposed to the dynamics of transference. The factors inherent in non-interference may be antithetical to the transference phenomenon. As one author put it:

> ...the concept of social work intervention may be consistent with much of the white man's culture, but it diametrically opposes the Native American's cultural concept of noninterference.[148]

In addition to the above, the factors of authority

and control affecting the social caseworker's professional view of self may be counterproductive in the therapeutic process with Native Americans. First of all, there is a built-it social work assumption that social workers must keep perspective, provide leadership, direction and have **authority** and **control** in the casework relationship; thus, many social workers may have been unable to follow the necessary intervention strategies adopted in the **Redthunder** case because they would have been required to give up authority and control. Another underlying assumption of the social casework profession is that "it is something I can do" as a professional that is responsible for the client's progress. However, in working with Native Americans, the social caseworker may not be designated as the "autonomous helper." Most of all, there is the view in the profession that it is the trained professional social caseworker who is most equipped to effectively modify a client's behavior; consequently, the notion of referring a case to a lay person is contrary to the social worker's professional self-concept and identity. The practice of social casework with Native Americans is contradictory to the basic foundation of social work education and theory.

It is apparent from the **Redthunder** case that the phenomenon of noninterference may be considered antithetical to the very essence of transference. The thesis of transference requires that the culture of a people reflect the cultural values and norms of the society in which the theory of transference originated. That is, the resolution of family and individual problems with the conscious and/or unconscious identification with significant others of the past must be functional. Nevertheless, it is inappropriate and against the intrinsic nature of the Native American culture for **others** to interfere. This is operational and functional within the Native American culture; consequently, there is no psychological need for Native Americans to develop a psyche attachment to a "significant other" within their past and transmit it to the worker in the present. The process of noninterference in the Native American culture impedes the need of individuals to identify with significant **others** as a means for establishing a self identity. This key variable must be understood and appreciated by the non-Indian world and non-Indian therapists in their work with Native Americans. As we have seen in the case of **Mrs. Redthunder,** it is possible through knowledge and use of Native American culture tradition to establish rapport and facilitate an effective resolution to the Native American social problem. It is clear, nonetheless, that one of the main ingredients of transference is the ability of the client to develop attachments with **significant others** and transfer those experiences to the worker. Somehow, in the transference process, the client irrationally responded to the therapist as though he/she were the **significant others** of the past. In the case of **noninterference** the notion of transference is stifled because the identity of **significant others** in the family and within the community do not play a key role in the psychi development of the Native American individual. There appears to be a philosophy of **psychi autonomy** in the Native American culture based on collective unity. In this instance the **psychi autonomy** (noninterference) world view suggests that the social identity of the individual is left primarily with internal strength. The cultural conformity is so designed that it supports this world view of **psychi autonomy** (noninterference) while at the same time fostering collective cohesion.

In the American culture it has become customary for individuals to attribute their social and psychological problems and development on the social dynamics of parents, siblings, community and **significant others.** Simply put, Western psychology supports the view that "you are the way you are because of your mother or father." Furthermore, transference is based on the principle that other individuals in the immediate environ-

170

ment serve as role models toward the maturation and development of the self. This emergence of self-identify through identification with **significant others** from a negative and/or positive perspective may cause difficulties and impairment in functioning later in life. However, the notion of **psychi autonomy** and **noninterference** in the Native American culture prohibits this process of transference. The values in the American Indian society are attached to the circular view of life whereby man is viewed as an extension of nature with the spiritual and non-spiritual forces of the universe having the paramount effects on the individual psyche. This is opposed to the cause-effect continuum prevalent in the American society that focuses on family, individual and environmental dynamics. These are important variables in understanding the relationship in therapy between worker and the Native American.

PUERTO RICANS: WORKER/CLIENT RELATIONSHIP

The Native American scholars state that they are probably the "most misunderstood" and "most stereotyped" of all minority groups. The Puerto Ricans, Mexican Americans and other People of Color may point to the dynamics of their relationship with the majority society and make the same statement. This factor of "who is the most oppressed," however, is destructive to the relationship between minorities and only serves to fragment minority interests. Minority group members seek **rewards** and **special treatment** from social programs based on "who is the most oppressed," and the different minority groups battle each other for that position of **oppression** rather than joining **collectively** to remove the oppression. The only **rewards** that can be derived from being the "most oppressed" and the "most stereotyped" are fatalistic in nature. In the same way that there is no "degree" of freedom, there is no "degree" of oppression, for both **freedom** and **oppression** are absolute. There is no

such thing as being "half-free" in the same manner that there is no such thing as being "half-
oppressed" or "most oppressed" and "more free."

The Puerto Ricans, as the Native Americans, are
divided into different tribes and ethnic groups
although there are similarities and commonalities
across ethnic lines. One author describes it
this way:

> The term "Latino" is used in this arti-
> cle as a generic label including all
> people of Spanish origin and descent.
> We maintain that Latinos may be thought
> of as members of a single cultural
> group in the sense that they share his-
> torically similarities in language,
> values, and tradition. Secondly, we
> simultaneously maintain that this
> Latino culture group is highly hetero-
> geneous, and that for some purposes,
> should be conceptualized as an aggre-
> gate of distinct subcultures, each pos-
> sessing a recognizable pattern of
> unique traits.[149]

Some of the cultural realities of the Puerto
Rican culture are as follows:

> Strong extended family relationships,
> which include godparents.[150]

> A high intrinsic value placed on **indi-
> vidualism** and/or **personalism**. These
> concepts are defined in a competitive
> sense in the United States, but in the
> Puerto Rican culture they are defined
> as safeguarding the inner integrity
> against group pressure and acquiring
> identity and self-confidence from the
> family.[151]

> An acceptance of the Divine Order of
> things as related to individual life.
> Many who have observed this phenomenon

172

have called it "fatalism" rather than viewing it from the Puerto Rican perspective of acknowledging and accepting the good and bad in life.[152]

Deference to authority figures.[153]

Patriarchal society with the woman playing a significant role as **counselor** in the personal lives of her children.[154]

Emphasis on the value of human relationships and contact over property and materialism.[155]

Emphasis on the strong male image where the male is regarded as assertive, aggressive and responsible for the well-being of the family while the female is the housekeeper and supporter of the male.[156]

The stature of manhood not attached to material worth but inherent in role definition.[157]

A strong belief in spiritualism and mysticism separating the cause-effect behavioral interpretation of life events.[158]

In-group cohesion of supporting one's own.[159]

Female virginity valued until marriage.[160]

Strict adherence to social amenities in personal relationships as well as their contact with professionals.[161]

A humanistic approach to life, both personal and business, with an emphasis on personalism, face-to-face contact.[162]

contact.[162]

Avoidance of confrontation with family members and others where one's feelings may be injured.[163]

As we look at the cultural realities of the Puerto Ricans and Native Americans, we are able to see many similarities. Many of the Puerto Ricans' and the Native Americans' cultural values are similar, such as a strong belief in the supernatural. Above all, the American stereotypes of Third World cultures are also similar. The Puerto Rican view of life as being destined by Supreme forces seems to suggest to the American culture that the Puerto Ricans are fatalistic. The Indian and Puerto Rican **deference** to **authority** may be looked at by Americans as docile and nonchalant in handling business affairs. The case illustration of **Mrs. D.** points out some of the significant factors involved in the Puerto Rican culture. According to the worker:

Mrs. D.'s mother used to pay for her grandson's boarding school tuition through the rental of part of her large house in Puerto Rico. Following the grandmother's death, Mrs. D. flew back to New York City from Puerto Rico, leaving all financial details to be worked out by her uncle because she was too grieved over the death of her mother to attend to these matters. Lacking the house rental income, she was forced to remove her son from the school where he had been doing well, she went to a therapist when her son began to act out after living in a slum area for the first time. The therapist discovered that it was the first time the child had acted out and the behavior was related to the boy's removal from the school where he had been happy. The therapist explored Mrs. D.'s fantasy and discovered that she had ex-

she had expected her uncle to continue
to rent part of the house without her
having to ask him; she was very good to
him and placed herself in his hands.
The therapist encouraged Mrs. D. to go
to Puerto Rico and confront her uncle
with the fact that as the only daughter, the house belonged to her. Nevertheless, the therapist understood why
she felt that she would have to wait
until her mother's birthday or anniver-
sary date of death.[164]

First of all, we can see the importance of the
extended family relationships in this Puerto Rican family. Secondly, the death of **Mrs. D.**'s mother resulted in a loss of money for her child's
schooling and her uncle was responsible for following through on the financial arrangements of
the insurance. However, he failed to do so. At
any rate, the therapist's knowledge about Puerto
Rican culture of "avoiding confrontations" with
family members and the supreme value placed on
family relationships enabled her to handle the
case appropriately. The worker did not apply the
American values of "individual property right"
and "you should confront your uncle with this."
A lack of cultural understanding of the Puerto
Rican culture on the part of the worker may have
resulted in the worker stimulating a confrontation between **Mrs. D.** and her uncle. This, of
course, would have left the client feeling that
the therapist "really didn't understand" and
would have hampered the therapeutic process.

On the other hand, the therapist may have possibly attributed to the client certain deep rooted
psychological problems related to passivity and
unresolved childhood experiences rather than engaging the authentic Puerto Rican cultural
dynamics. Such an attitude on the part of the
worker as "fight for what is rightfully yours" in
abolishing **passivity** of the client could only
have resulted in creating more psychological
problems for the client. It is the unawareness

and insensitivity of the caseworker to the Third World culture that may be responsible for provoking countertransference in therapy.

Needless to say, any worker, Puerto Rican or otherwise, who is trained in professional schools of social work today is destined to be insensitive to Puerto Ricans and other People of Color because (1) curriculum materials relating to People of Color are sparse and (2) the process of therapy is based on American cultural values. Third World minority social workers may be keenly aware from personal experiences as well as subjective emotions that "this theory does not apply to my race/ethnic group." However, in order to demonstrate their competence, Third World minority students are educated into following the dictates of their academic training rather than accepting their emotional reaction. Also, there is the usual ambivalence on the part of the minority worker to deny and/or accept the academic proposition. There is a need of the minority worker to accept the theory of the social sciences on minority culture because "they must know" and the minority workers minimize their personal knowledge by saying, "What do I know, I'm just speaking from personal experience." Yet, there is a desire of the practitioner to question the social science foundation and to explore new theoretical constructs in order to facilitate new models of intervention. In most cases, the Third World minority practitioners are asked by the theorists to accept **intellectually** what they feel **emotionally** to be quite the contrary. On the other hand, there are minority workers who reject their own culture and identify with the **mainstream** culture in terms of what they conceive to be "American" and "white middle class." In this instance, it is easy for such workers to become insensitive to their culture and racial/ethnic group or to seek alternative models for therapy. The case of **Mrs. D.** was resolved in the following manner:

Dealing with Mrs. D.'s passive dependency without finding an immediate way to restore the equilibrium would not be helpful. In Puerto Rico, conflict or confrontation with family members must be avoided at all costs; particularly when an elder or money is involved. Recognizing the cultural implications of the situation, the therapist first informed Mrs. D. that she was the legal heir and then encouraged her to take her two children with her in order to get public opinion on her side and thus pressure the uncle to relent.[165]

As in the previous case of **Mrs. Redthunder,** a Native American, we will see unorthodox social casework practices being applied to accommodate the cultural factors of Puerto Rican clients. The added barriers that the ethnic/cultural component play in such therapeutic situations prohibit the effective utilization of the worker in the therapeutic encounter. Consequently, the role of the worker is stifled by having to relinquish the task of traditional **helper.** Most of all, the worker may be hampered by lack of knowledge on ethnic/racial cultures.

A case illustration that demonstrates the inappropriate application of the therapeutic process with Puerto Ricans through overlooking significant aspects of the Puerto Rican culture is as follows:

Marta was in group therapy for six months and was beginning to transfer her loyalties to her peer group as well as to the mental health professionals in the clinic. Many of the group members openly mocked Marta's strong belief in virginity and even conveyed the impression that a man who still wanted to marry a virgin had something wrong with him. This reaction had less of an effect on Marta than the implied value

judgment of the therapists when they
asked the same questions after hearing
she had a boyfriend: "Are you having
sexual relations with him?" "Why not?"
Because of the therapists authority
roles and questions, Marta perceived a
message that said, "there's something
wrong." A little later, the therapist
and group members were extremely sur-
prised by Marta's unwed pregnancy, so
unlike her and so opposite to the
strong convictions she had displayed
earlier.[166]

If the group worker had been aware of (1) the
strong value in the traditional Puerto Rican culture on female virginity until marriage, (2) the
belief of individualism in maintaining one's
ideas without peer influence and (3) the deference to authority, this situation could have been
avoided. The worker could have used the information on Puerto Rican culture to assist other members in the group to understand the uniqueness
of **Marta** and her culture. In this way, there
could have been the development of mutual respect
between group members and the avoidance of an unwed pregnancy that, most surely, must have created other problems for **Marta** in her home and environment.

The **deference to authority** is clearly manifested
in the **Marta** case in that the mere question of
"why not" was an indicator for **Marta** of approval
from the authority figure. The response of the
worker may have served as an impetus for the
client's actions given the respect and **deference**
of the Puerto Ricans to the authority.

The recurring theme of cultural conflict as opposed to factors of racism is most prevalent in
the cases involving Native Americans, Puerto Rican and Mexican Americans who migrate into this
society are survival on low income, inadequate
housing and poverty. Above all, these Third
World minority individuals are con-

cerned about being perceived as poor, unworthy and helpless. Yet, they bring with them values of pride, respect and honor.

Let us turn our attention to a more complex case illustration as it highlights other dimensions of Puerto Rican culture in the worker relationship with Puerto Ricans. This case illustration provides an in-depth social history and a dramatizing of the intervention of a social caseworker practitioner:

> **Juan** and **Carmen R.** live in a tenement in the South Bronx. They have five children, three sons born in Puerto Rico and two daughters born in the United States. Juan was previously employed as a clerk in a New York City grocery store or **bodega.** He completed an eighth grade education in a small interior town in Puerto Rico but was unable to attend high school in the city because his parents, who had twelve children, could not afford the necessary shoes, uniforms,and transportation. Instead, Juan began working full time along side his father in the **finca** (farm) of the wealthy L. family. Juan asked God to forgive him for his envious thoughts toward his brother Jose, who was the godson of Senor L. and had his tuition paid by the wealthy farmer. Juan's own godparents were good to him and remembered all the occasions and feasts, but they were poor. When Juan was sixteen, his godfather, Pedro, got him a job on the pineapple farm of the coastal city of Arecibo. He enjoyed living with Pedro's family. At age twenty-four he fell in love with Pedro's granddaughter, Carmen, who was sixteen, in the tenth grade, and a virgin. Apart from family gatherings and Sundays in the plaza, however, he was unable to see her. Finally, he asked

179

her father for her hand in marriage and
the latter consented because he thought
of Juan as a brother. The patron
loaded his **finca** for the wedding and
contributed a roasted pig for the oc-
casion. Over fifty people from infancy
to age ninety were there to celebrate
the wedding.

Juan was very proud when his first born
was a son but his pride as a man was
hurt when Carmen had to return to work
as a seamstress because of the increasing debts. Her family took care of the
baby and fought over who would be the
godparents. By the time a third child
was born, a show of God's blessing,
Juan was let go at the pineapple farm
and he and his family moved to San
Juan, where his brother, Jose, got him
a job in a supermarket. This job did
not last long and after a long period
of unemployment and health problems
with the youngest child, Juan moved to
New York City with Carmen's brother,
who obtained for him the job in the
bodega.

Carmen was delighted with being reuni-
ted with her family, but when she became pregnant with their fourth child,
the R.'s moved into their own apartment. Carmen became depressed because
for the first time she was not living
with extended family, because of the
stress of the change of culture, because of her inability to speak English, and because of the deterioration
of the tenement which was impossible to
keep sparkling clean. She suffered
from headaches, stomach problems, and
pains in her chest, but doctors told
her these symptoms were due to nerves
and her condition was chronic. When
she felt better she would raise the

volume of the **jibaro** music on the Spanish station and talk to her saints.
Juan sent for Carmen's aunt to come to
live with them and her arrival helped
Carmen.   Carmen accepted Juan's argu-
ments that in America, jobs, schooling,
and medical facilities were better than
in Puerto Rico. (In some ways the job
and medical facilities in Puerto Rico
were nonexistent unless one had a car.)
The years passed and Carmen consoled
herself that as soon as the children
finished their education they would
move back to Puerto Rico where Juan
could set up a business. As the children grew they adopted the ways of the
neighborhood children.   They no longer
asked for their parent's blessing as
they came and left the house; they wanted to go to parties unchaperoned; they
sometimes talked back; the girls wanted
to wear make-up at age fifteen and
dress in non-ladylike clothes.   The
boys had friends who belonged to gangs
and smoked pot, and the parents feared
the same would happen to their sons.
Juan and Carmen threatened to send them
back to Puerto Rico or to a **colegio**
(boarding school) if they did not sever
these friendships.

Another important and traumatic issue
that the family faced for the first
time involved the issue of color. The
youngest daughter, Yvette, age twelve,
entered junior high school and found
herself placed on the black side of the
two camps in school.   This situation
affected the entire family.   Carmen reminded her daughter that she was a
Puerto Rican and told her to speak
Spanish loudly so the school children
would not confuse her with the Blacks.
Inside, Carmen felt guilty that her
daughter's dark skin led to problems.

During this very difficult period Juan injured his back while loading merchandise and became permanently disabled. Suddenly, the family had to receive public welfare assistance, and Juan's authority was gradually becoming undermined, particularly as he was no longer the breadwinner. He began to drink. Trips to Puerto Rico, while somewhat supportive, did not provide a solution to the problems the family was undergoing. Finally, Yvette came to the attention of school authorities because of her withdrawn behavior and she was referred to a mental health center.[167]

Here we see: (1) the significance that god-parents play in the extended family; (2) the role that immediate family members play in the extended family, such as acquiring a job for a family member; (3) the value of virginity in the marriage of Juan and Carmen; (4) the role conflict created when Carmen, the wife, had to go to work rather than stay at home as housekeeper, which is valued in the culture; (5) the anxiety created due to inability to live with extended family during Carmen's pregnancy; (6) the experienced conflict in clash of cultures with the rearing of children; (7) the experienced racism due to darker color of youngest daughter and, finally, (8) a shift in definition of a male role due to the loss of job and the resulting low self-esteem, which led to alcoholism.

In the case of cultural conflict and the underlying factors of racism in this case, the first criteria for effective therapy is to recognize the cultural component rather than attributing the behavior of the client and family members to some unrelated psychodynamic factors. Secondly, there should be acceptance, appreciation, awareness and sensitivity to the Puerto Rican culture. Thirdly, there is a need to assist the client (in this case family) in being able to see the relationship of the presenting problem to the cultural phenomenon when exploring some internal psychological problem. Fourthly, the worker's awareness of Puerto Rican culture and all its manifestations should be included into the therapeutic intervention process. For example, in the case of **Mrs. D.**, the Puerto Rican female who avoided confrontation with her uncle, it would have been insensitive for the worker to deny the Puerto Rican cultural dynamics and to provoke a confrontation. The very nature of the worker's attempt to use her "authority" to do this would have been in opposition to the nature of the Puerto Rican cultural realm. If there is a violation of Puerto Rican culture on the part of the worker in attempting to bring about a solution that individual and/or family members face, such action defeats the purpose for which the therapy is intended.

Therefore, the ultimate goal of any worker in the case of **Carmen** and **Juan** should be an attempt to get this family to look at the cultural psychosocial dynamics that they face in the same way that traditional social casework utilized the psychosocial model to attempt to get the client to see the psychological factors that may be inhibiting his/her functioning. Finally, the worker should utilize the client's knowledge of his/her culture as clues to the possibilities for resolution of the presenting problem. Due to the significance of the "counselor's role" that mothers play in the Puerto Rican family dynamics, the worker should include possibilities of including the mother of Carmen in the therapeutic process.

Even though there appears to be an intensified emphasis on the significance of culture in therapy with members of ethnic/racial minorities, the caseworker must also be sensitive to the fact that there are Puerto Ricans, Native Americans, Mexican Americans and Blacks who view themselves as having successfully assimilated into the American culture. Therefore, they may deny their ethnicity and racial identification and, at the same time, deny that their difficulties are in any way related to their culture and ethnicity.

At this point, the worker is not to "throw away the book" on the cultural realities of such an individual or family and begin immediately to employ the techniques available for white middle class American clients. At the same time, the worker is not to totally abolish concerns about the relationship between the client's ethnic identity and the problems presented. There have been numerous case illustrations to demonstrate the significance of race on the presenting problem though denied by the client. In fact, the issue of race may be the core of the problem. Consequently, the question of culture should always be prevalent in the same manner that the question of race is prevalent in the Black/white relationship. In the same way that the therapist must explore the relevance of race when there is a difference in racial make-up of worker and client, the same principles must apply in the relationship between worker and client of different cultural make-up.

MEXICAN-AMERICAN: WORKER/CLIENT RELATIONSHIP

The Mexican-American is victimized by the American systems in the same ways as Blacks, Puerto Ricans and Native Americans. Although each minority has had its unique psycho-historical relationship with the majority race, the results appear to be very much the same. As we look at some of the dymanics of the effects of contemporary oppression and colonization in the Mexican-American society, we will find the following:

Deficient educational achievement due to the lack of educational opportunities.

Excessive unemployment.

Broken homes.

Excessive numbers of police in Mexican-

American communities.

Police-community friction.

The overrepresentation of Mexican-Americans in jails and prisions for offenses related to drinking and drugs.

The gross lack of mental health treatment facilities in Mexican-American communities.

The general unavailability of psychiatric manpower, particularly bilingual mental health professionals.

Societal resistance toward the funding of community mental health centers directed by and under Mexican American community control and sanction.[168]

The mere substitution of the concept **Mexican-American** for **Puerto Rican, Native American** and **Black** or any other Third World minority group and the same variables above would apply. The observation of the above dynamics in the minds of the majority race in America serves as support and justification for many of the negative stereotypes, prejudices and assumptions that exist creating a vicious perpetual cycle. In most cases, it is the discrimination and prejudices of white America that are responsible for the conditions cited above, and the negative responses by minorities to these conditions are used by the majority race to discriminate further and thus justify the stereotypes. Hugh Butts' illustration on Black-white relations is useful here:

The definition of Blacks as violent, inferior, promiscuous and irresponsible has given rise to certain institutions that serve to perpetuate these definitions.

Thus, if Black people are defined as

185

violent, police practices are encouraged that provoke violent group reaction among Black people.[169]

A prime example may be observed in large areas
where Third World minorities live. More often
than not, there is an unusually large patrol of
police reinforcements in those minority areas the
white society define as violent, whereas the presence of the mass police patrol may be the very
factor that provokes violence in those areas.

In the area of the worker/client relationship,
minorities may be defined as nonverbal and resis-
tive to psychotherapy techniques, but it may be
the failure of the worker to be creative and
effective in the therapeutic process by utilizing
the cultural variables of People of Color. Yet,
the lack of creativity on the part of the worker
often serves as support and justification for the
worker's assumption that it is the fault of the
minorities.

As one resource puts it, mankind over the years
has formed cohesive groups based on color and
insanity. In the case of Mexican-Americans and
other People of Color, they are faced with double
jeopardy when confronted with an emotional problem and being People of Color at the same time.
In fact, there is little separation from being
"crazy" and being Mexican-American. In the
American culture being Mexican and being "crazy"
are synonymous. One client responded to the difficulties experienced with white institutions by
saying "we are not ignorant and dumb."

In a review of the literature it is apparent that
Mexican-Americans and others who have a **native
tongue** are very sensitive about the barriers that
language differences play in their interaction
with non-Spanish institutions and systems for
receiving social services.[170]

The importance of the impact of language on the
English/non-English speaking worker/client rela-

tionship is best illustrated in the following Mexican-American's contact with a worker who could speak Spanish:

> It was suggested that Mrs. X. ask her husband if he could come with her to the center. She agreed to do so and to call back later in the evening when her husband came home from work, adding, 'It is good to talk to someone who can speak Spanish.[171]

A further elaboration on the significance of language is recorded in the words of another client.

> On the other hand, if a person does not speak the dominant language, he is harassed, punished, or ignored. Chicano clients who did not speak English explained to this writer during the initial interview that previous visits from non-Chicano social workers had been upsetting experiences for them. The social workers had not spoken Spanish and had made the client feel guilty and inferior because she knew no English. Whenever the social worker came, one of her small children had to be sent to a neighbor's home to ask for someone to serve as interpreter for her.[172]

It is only through the experience of Mexican-American clients that we can fully understand the dynamics of language, culture and racial differences as a barrier in the worker/client relationship. In addition to the stereotypes and "put downs" from just being "Mexican," there is the added harassment and abuse for speaking a different language. It is easy to identify the negative implication on the therapeutic process of having a translator who may be a neighbor or the **client's** child. The effective mastery of the English language in the minds of English speakers is somehow associated with one's degree of intelligence and/or acculturation one has adopted to the Americans' values and to the American system. The assumption seems to be that "the better one is able to master English," the more intelligent and upwardly mobile one is. It is the association of the English language with superiority and any other languages with inferiority that may contribute to the condescension and resulting harassment of the Mexican-American and other non-English speaking clients. This harassment, whether intentional or nonintentional, creates the same negative results of devaluating the client. It is difficult to separate the language of a people from the culture and way of life of a people. The language they speak is an integral part of who they are in that language influences culture and culture influences language. Yet, it is practically impossible to provide all Mexican-American clients with Spanish-speaking Mexican-American workers, and this is not even suggested. However, the severity of the problem of insensitivity to the language of Mexican-Americans and other People of Color on the part of the worker must be highlighted and recognized.

Although language differences appear to be a barrier in worker/client interaction with Mexican-Americans, the lack of understanding of the Mexican-American culture is another major component. The Mexican-American is no less bombarded with a barrage of stereotypes and misunderstandings than any other minority. There appears to be consensus in the literature on the following realities of the Mexican-Americans that may be pertinent to the issue of psychotherapy:

Strong extended family relationships.

An acceptance of the Divine order of things as related to their individual lives and to the fate impaired on them.

Deference to authority figures.

188

Patriarchal society with the female playing the needed role of housekeeper and supporter of husband.

Emphasis on the strong male image.

A strong belief in the spiritualism and mysticism.

In-group cohesion of supporting one's own.

Adherence to socializing and 'getting to know' prior to meaningful discussion.

Loyalty to nationhood.

Strong influence of religion in their lives.

The initial contact between the worker and a client of Mexican-American origin is crucial to the development of rapport, trust and confidence. This initial contact will determine the effectiveness of therapy and the outcome of the therapeutic process. The relevance of the initial contact as a component in Mexican-American culture will be illustrated in the following case:

Family X is made up of the parents and three children: a girl 6 years old and two boys, ages 7 and 16. Mr. and Mrs. X were legally married at one time, but because of serious marital problems and pressures from Mrs. X's family, they were divorced three years ago. However, they managed to resolve their problems and came together again; the church never considered them divorced. The family lives in a small house in the back of a large empty lot that has not been taken care of properly. Weeds have taken over the majority of the land so that they conceal the house.

The probation department referred Family X to the community center because neither the father nor the mother were able to communicate in English. The probation officer explained that this family needed counseling and also 'someone who could speak their language.' The parents were unable to control their 16-year old son, Freddy, who had been placed on probation for running away from home regularly.

Mrs. X. had been told to call the center for an appointment. This might have been sufficient to start the helping process for an Anglo-Saxon Protestant family; for a Mexican American family it was not.

Not only was it difficult for the family to overcome the shame of having to deal with the law, but Mr. X. who made all the decisions -- had been disregarded by the probation officer. It was decided that establishing contact was up to the center, on the assumption that this would be difficult or impossible for Mrs. X.

The director of the community center called Mrs. X., identifying himself in Spanish as a social worker who knew that her son had been in some trouble, and explained that the center was a voluntary not a governmental agency.[173]

The social process of "getting acquainted" as an **initial step** is prohibited in traditional casework practice. It must be understood that this "small talk," which is advocated with Mexican American clients, must be **genuine** and **authentic**. The importance of **authenticity** and **sincerity** is just as important as **acceptance** and **individualization** as underlying principles of the casework relationship.

Another element of importance to recognize in social casework with Mexican Americans is their **deference to authority** accompanied with their **suspiciousness** of the American institutions. Recognizing this factor, the worker applied the technique of contacting the family rather than having the family to make the contact. Again, it is customary in traditional social work practice that the responsibility for making contacts with the agency is left with the client. The failure of clients to seek agencies on their own results in their being defined as "culturally disadvantaged" and victims of "cultural lag." **Suspiciousness** and **distrust** of institutions are generic to all minorities. We see the following as the case of **Mr. & Mrs. X.** continues:

> Mr. and Mrs. X. came to the center for the interview. True to Latin custom, the first hour was leisurely. They talked mainly about familiar things that they could comfortably share with the worker. Conversation centered around Mexico, where they had lived until about two years before. They shared information about their respective families and mentioned how difficult it was for them to get used to the American way of life. Here they had no close relatives nearby to whom they could turn when problems arose. It was disconcerting for them to have to bother people outside the family.[174]

This **initial**, informal "leisurely sharing" with a client during therapy may appear threatening to a worker who is trained to **keep perspectives.** The Mexican American client, as other People of Color, requires innovative therapeutic techniques. A minority client is much more apt to view the worker with **trust** and **confidence** if the cultural dimension of the client's life is taken under consideration. The Mexican American client is able to see the worker developing an interest in him/her as an individual through the use of "getting acquainted" as opposed to the "make-believe" approach of "getting acquainted."

Another cultural element specific to the Mexican American culture and generic to other minority cultures is the commonality of viewing social and personal problems as being somehow attributed to a Divine Power. There is a strong belief in a Supreme Being, who has a direct influence on the psychological and/or physical fate of a person. At the same time there is the view that others may be able to use the working of spiritual forces to alleviate social and psychological problems. In traditional Mexican society, certain social and physical illnesses are associated with supernatural dynamics foreign to Western culture. First of all, there is **Mal ojo**, translated to mean "bad eye." According to one of the authorities on the subject:

> **Mal ojo**, literally translated "bad eye," is believed to be a result of excessive admiration or desire on the part of another person. Symptoms indicative of this illness are sleepiness, a general malaise, and frequently, a severe headache. The recommended treatment is to find the person who has cast the **mal ojo** (usually unintentionally) and have him manually caress the victim. **Mal ojo** is not generally interpreted as a consequency of evil intention.[175]

Another concept of illness in the Mexican culture is **Mal de Susto**, translated to mean "illness from fright." Following is a description of the illness, method of cure and a case illustration:

> **Mal de susto**, literally translated "illness from fright," is a syndrome believed to be the result of an emotional traumatic experience. Basic symptoms include restlessness during

sleep, feelings of listlessness, loss of energy, and occasionally, night sweats. **Susto** is part of a complex set of beliefs in which the individual is thought to be composed of a corporal being and one or more immaterial souls or spirits that may become detached from the body and wander freely. In **Mal de susto** the individual is believed to have experienced a soul loss. In the process of coaxing the soul back to the corporal being, the patient is massaged and often sweated. He is also swept or rubbed with some object to remove the illness from the body.[176]

On a Sunday outing, Ricardo, the older boy (five years old) suffered an attack of **Susto**. The rest of the family romped in and about the water of a local pond, but Ricardo demurred. Despite coaxing and taunts, especially from his seven-year old sister, Ricardo would have nothing to do with the water, but climbed into the automobile and went to sleep. He slept throughout the afternoon and did not even awake when he was taken home after dark and put to bed. That night he slept fitfully and several times talked aloud in his sleep. On the following morning, the parents decided that Ricardo had suffered a **susto**. It was caused, they reasoned, not by fear of the water but by the family's insistence that he enter the pond -- a demand to which he was unable to accede. They brought him to a local center to have his soul coaxed back to his body, and thus, be healed of soul loss.[177]

There are other unique examples of illnesses, and "folk" cure practices, but we will limit the discussion here only to the cases that are essential and relevant. The following case illustration is between a folk healer and a Mexican American client:

> **Mal puesto**, or sorcery, is considered a consequence of one of three kinds of social relationships: a lover's quarrel, an unrequited affair, or a reflection of invidiousness between individuals or nuclear families. Dramatic mania is a characteristic symptom of **Mal puesto**. When mania is present, the individual is aware that he is possessed by another individual. **Mal puesto** is characterized by its chronicity and unresponsiveness to cure of any kind.

> A young woman described a case in which the victim, who was one of her acquaintances, failed to return the affection of a suitor. He, aware of her lack of interest, offered her an orange soda. After drinking the soda she became demented **(se volvia loca)**, surely he had placed something in her soda **(echo algo)**. Her face turned colors, her eyebrows drew tightly together, and her eyes became huge; she was, in fact, a very ugly sight. She had an appetite only for orange soda; all other food was rejected because of her suspicion that it contained hairs and insects **(cabellos and animalitos)**. Her nights became sleepless nightmares because of the dogs and turkeys which she thought crawled upon, leaped, kicked and bruised her body. Inasmuch as only she was aware of those creatures, her family proved powerless to protect her despite their concern. On the mornings following such attacks she arose covered by bruises and other marks of her anguished travails. She was taken from one healer to another; from **curandero** to physician, physician to **curandero**,

without respite and to no avail.[178]

According to the literature, another term used alternately with **mal puesto** is **brujeria** (witchcraft). Oftentime, such illness brought on by witchcraft is alleviated. It is common in the Third World culture to hear tales of how one was "fixed" (witchcrafted) and/or how one was successful in "getting the 'fix' off them." There have been reports that spiritualists and witch doctors succeeded in alleviating a "fix" while medical doctors failed to provide a cure.

Much of the practice of **voodoo** or witchcraft is associated with the supernatural and the Third World of Africa. One need not eat or drink something planted by an enemy to cause harm or injury, but harm can be accomplished through supernatural forces, such as placing certain herbs or artifacts in a person's surroundings. As in the case above, difficulties in personal relationships can also be caused by witchcraft. It is the understanding of these dynamics that the casework practitioner must be sensitive to as they relate to the Mexican American client. Let us look at the case of **Miss L.**

> Miss L., in her late thirties, was unmarried and lived alone in the **barrio**. She had been referred to the agency by a Spanish speaking community organization worker after she had been injured at work and could no longer receive unemployment compensation benefits. Miss L. had emigrated from Mexico with her parents when she was a young girl, and she eventually settled in Detroit. Both parents had been dead several years. Her siblings manifested serious psychiatric problems, and one sister, diagnosed as schizophrenic, had long been hospitalized.
>
> Miss L. had devoted her early years to providing a livelihood for her younger

siblings; now that they were all married or living away from home, she found herself alone. Her only outlet was a few church activities. She was frequently depressed and suffered from several psychosomatic illnesses. Underlying the depression was unresolved Oedipal conflict and rage toward her parents and siblings for responsibilities placed on her. Even when she recognized some of these feelings, **Miss L continued symbolically to express rage against relatives and siblings who were still making emotional demands on her – demands that she provoked.** She found herself responding through psychosomatic symptoms that tended to undermine her well-being.

The short-range goal was to establish a casework relationship and to attempt to diagnose her problems. Miss L accepted referral only because the referral came from a Spanish-speaking community organization worker whom she respected and who, in essence, depended on her for carrying out church-related social project.[179]

As we review Third World case illustrations, we will find that the Mexican-Americans usually get to a social agency via referral from other Mexicans whom they respect, such as priests and spiritualists. We also see the importance that religion and church play in the lives of the Mexican-Americans. The only "outlet" for **Miss L** was her church acctivities. Finally, we see the symptoms of depression and loneliness experienced by the client due to the separation from siblings whom she raised and the emotional demands being made on her by family members as an indication of extended family life in Mexican-American culture.

It was the immediate response of the therapist to look at the problem with **Miss L** in the context

ior in one culture may be totally inappropriate
for another culture. Clients understand their
behavior from a cultural context, and the therapist's lack of recognition of those variables is
an acknowledgement by the client that the therapist does not understand despite his/her verba-
lizing of "I understand." In this context the
therapist may be understanding the wrong thing.

A final case illustration of the Mexican-American
experience with a psychotherapist will highlight
many other diversified variables.

>Mrs. C is a 30-year-old Spanish-
>American. Her parents were born in a
>small village in the San Luis Valley in
>southern Colorado. She had two older
>sisters and a younger brother and sis-
>ter. Like many of my patients, this
>patient's original language was Span-
>ish. She learned English in school in
>a poor, but then largely white neigh-
>borhood in Denver to which the family
>moved when the patient was five. The
>patient and her siblings finished high
>school. The patient married a Spanish-
>American construction worker five years
>before seeking therapy. The C's have
>two children, a girl four and a boy
>three, and live in a single home.
>
>Mrs. C has never seen a psychiatrist
>before. She came to the clinic because
>of "loneliness" of two months' duration
>and difficulty in swallowing of one
>month's duration. She related the on-
>set of her loneliness to an incident at
>a family gathering. Her brother ac-
>cused her of insulting his second wife,
>and her father agreed. The patient's
>husband defended her, eventually knock-
>ing her father down. Although they all
>made up two days later, the patient be-

gan to feel lonely and worried. She became sensitive to her husband's change in job hours, which kept him away from home more than usual, and especially sensitive to her husband's usual habit of staying out with the boys.

One Sunday afternoon a month before she saw me, her husband was late and the family had to rush to Church. Her husband drove in an aggressive way, frightening her, and once there the children were noisy. That evening the patient had the fear she would not be able to swallow, and in fact, could not.

Before her appointment to begin outpatient treatment, on her mother's advice the patient had gone in search of a traditional Spanish healer. For reasons that were not clear, she could not find one. When asked if she had had some reluctance to come to the clinic, she replied, "Let people think what they will. I know not only crazy people come here."

Before her second visit, she called to say that she felt worse and asked if I would hypnotize her. By the time of the session she had recalled what preceded this exacerabation. Her husband had come home late again. She wondered if he purposefully wanted to upset her. As she said this, she fingered her crucifix. She sadly told of her loneliness as a child because of greater attention given to the older and younger siblings. She then changed the subject and talked about an Anglo teacher who had slapped her unfairly when she was ten. There had been only two or three other Spanish children in

199

the school, and they were also abused. At this point she sounded angry; however, she returned to the subject of the numerous unpleasant experiences in her own family due to 'unfair' treatment at the hands of her parents and siblings. She spoke of how lonely she had been because of her husband's long hours away from home. When I asked her if she was angry about this, she gulped, drooled saliva, and said 'no.'

In the next hour, she spoke again about her experiences with Anglos. She described her bravery in telling one Anglo boy to shut up when she was still a girl. She said that she had 'stood up' to a rude police chief on whom she had waited in a restaurant where she worked. He later apologized, and she accepted this; however, he died shortly afterward of a heart attack. She had visible difficulty swallowing at this point and attempted to change the subject. Was she afraid of her anger? She admitted that she had feared her anger might have caused his death. She then described another incident, of police brutality involving her brother, and how she had come to his assistance. The police had been so impressed by her stand that an officer was sent to apologize. He stated that his offending colleague had mistakenly 'thought you were just another dumb Mexican.' Soon after that, she had been involved in a traffic accident. Though she wondered if she was being punished for her anger, she was also happy since she said, 'I learned to open my mouth.'

She soon reported improvement in her swallowing. She made her husband change his hours and had warned him: 'If you go back to your old routine,

I'll get worse.' Her children were also better behaved. She began to speak of the possible background for her particular symptom. Eating had always presented a special problem for her. Her father used meal times to criticize. Her mother would hide information from him to keep him from getting angry at the table. The patient would avoid her father, she told me as she gulped.

She said she had tended to deny being angry since childhood; her mother had always held it against her father for being such a disagreeable, angry person. Her mother had suffered from trouble swallowing during the first years of her own marriage. At the suggestion of a traditional healer, she had relatives stay with her, since the healer felt she was lonely, and she was cured.

During the sixth hour the patient brought up the possibility of terminating treatment. At the next session, however, she said that she had been irritated at first when I agreed to terminate, because she felt she might not be ready. She had had a difficult week because her husband had started a business partnership with her father and brother, of which she did not approve. When she recognized her anger, she said to herself, 'Don't get upset,' and she had not developed trouble in swallowing. Instead, she had made her opinion clear to her husband. She thus felt that she had accomplished what she had set out to do in therapy and felt ready to terminate.[180]

Let us review some of the obvious signs and

demonstrations of Mexican-American culture in this case:

> Role of the spiritualist (folk healer).
>
> Associating of Mexican-Americans with being crazy. ("Let people think what they will. I know that not only crazy people come here.")
>
> Significance of religion. ("As she said this she fingered her crucifix.")
>
> Associating "being dumb" with being Mexican-American. ("The patient was 'too dumb to tell' her mother.") And the stereotype of white society of Mexican-Americans as "dumb."
>
> Anger at white Americans and American institutions.
>
> Negative contact with authorities (policemen).

A key aspect to the therapeutic relationship overlooked by the therapist is the significance that food plays in the cultural lives of the Mexican-Americans. There is no mention of **Empacho,** which is associated with clinging of food to the wall of the stomach. As one author puts it:

> ...**empacho** is caused by a complex interaction of social and psysiological forces. It is most likely to result in a citation in which another individual is allowed to override one's personal autonomy.[181]

This is exactly what happened in the case of **Mrs. C.** The client had overridden her personal autonomy with others including her father, husband and authorities by her forceful behavior. Nonetheless, the significant factors played up by the therapist were:

> Sibling rivalry based on older and youngest getting more attention than she.

> Unfair treatment from parents.

> Hostile father.

> Client's anger.

> Father used mealtime to criticize.

All of the psychosocial data highlighted in this case illustrate the typical orientation of Western psychology, which related psychological problems to unresolved envy of other siblings, conflicts with parents and overidentification with a particular parent. The client's experience with this data somehow gets transferred to the therapist, who serves as the objective entity to resolve the conflict. She was being asked to "stomach something" that she had difficulty in digesting psychologically, such as an overbearing husband and father.

In conclusion, the material presented in this section substantiates even further the need to include the cultural variable of the Third World minority cultures. It is the recognition of the unique cultural differences of minorities and the specifics of how they apply to particular groups that will facilitate the therapeutic process. The absence of the recognition of cultural differences may be destructive to the therapeutic relationship.

IMPLICATION OF SOCIAL CASEWORK WITH NATIVE
AMERICANS, PUERTO RICANS AND MEXICAN-AMERICANS

There are a few dynamics that social work practitioners must realize in the therapeutic practice with Third World minority clients. In most in-

stances it is not important as to whether the
worker is a member of the dominant society or
whether he/she is a member of a minority group
being served. The same principles must apply.
Some of these principles are as follows:

Recognition of the unique cultural
traits of each ethnic minority group as
it pertains to the delivery of services.

Appreciation and sensitivity of unique
cultural traits within each minority
group.

Recognition and appreciation for the
element of distrust when manifested in
contact with Third World minority
clients.

Early exploration in the therapeutic
process of the meaning of the differences in ethnicity, race, and culture.

Recognition and acceptance of "not
knowing it all" but expression of a
willingness to learn about Third World
cultures.

Sensitivity and awareness of the unique
conflicts that may exist between the
worker's ethnic group and the minority
ethnic group being helped.

Recognition and acceptance that
European theories of human behavior may
not be adequate for understanding the
behavior of the particular minority
group being helped.

Use of the social dynamics and parameters inherent in a specific minority
culture to resolve problems of personal
adjustment.

Appreciation of and a willingness to learn the language of the minority culture being helped.

Looking at each Third World minority client as an individual and not as a reflection of what "you might subjectively think" about that specific minority group.

Use and understanding of the minority client's cultural definition and significance of his/her social and psychological problem as a measure for treatment.

Awareness and recognition of linguistic interpretation of a minority group's use of symbols and words as they may differ from the dominant society, even though the same words may be used.

Recognition that culture is fluent, changing and not static; therefore, there must be a readiness to constantly assess and reassess and maintain a flexible view of culture in relationship to the therapeutic process.

IMPLICATION FOR SELECTED ORIENTAL AMERICAN ETHNIC GROUPS

The focus on Oriental minorities will be limited to general cultural characteristics of Chinese-Americans, Japanese-Americans and Koreans. The generic cultural patterns that exist among all Third World cultures mentioned above are:

Distrust and suspicion of strangers.

Deference to an authority regime that may impede self-disclosure of certain material that may appear confrontative.

Taking care of their own personal problems within internal family structure.

The value of noninterference from others within and without their society.

Fear of not being totally accepted due to their unique ways and customs.

Experienced conflicts with external world due to unique customs and life style.

Suspiciousness and distrustfulness of the American establishments and institutions.

Getting acquainted with a person before revealing self.

Each of the Oriental-American minorities mentioned above share the following specific cultural traits:

Under-utilization of mental health facilities, such as mental health clinics, family service centers and mental hospitals.

Adoption of a general low-profile in addressing the American institution of perjudice, discrimination and racism.

Strong emphasis on educational and vocational achievement.

Custom of handling problems within the family.

Respect and obedience to parents and to elders.

Motivation to achieve success in order to please family and family name.

Valuing self-control and inhibition of strong feelings.

Although the above may be considered the general commonalities that exist among Oriental-Americans mentioned, there are some exceptions to this rule. Koreans usually exhibit the following characteristics:

An attitude of trust combined with vigilance in relationship with others.

Emphasis on the value of endurance and moderation.

Combined ambivalence of humility and assertiveness.

Appearing to perform better as individuals than as groups.

133. Ronald G. Lewis and Man Keung Ho, "Social Work with Native Americans," _Social Work_, (September, 1975.)

134. Jimm G. Good Tracks, "Native American Noninterference," _Social Work_, (November, 1973).

135. Herbert H. Locklear, "Native American Myths," _Social Work_, (May, 1972), _See also_: Ronald G. Lewis and Keung Ho, "Social work with Native Americans," _Social Work_, (September, 1975).

136. Jimm G. Good Tracks, "Native American Noninterference," _Social Work_, (November, 1973).

137. Herbert H. Locklear, "Native American Myths," _Social Work_, (May, 1972).

138. Jimm G. Good Tracks, "Native American Noninterference," _Social Work_, (November, 1973).

139. Ronald G. Lewis and Keung Ho, "Social Work with Native Americans," _Social Work_, (September, 1975).

140. Jimm G. Good Tracks, "Native American Noninterference," _Social Work_, (November, 1973).

141. Ibid.

142. Ibid.

143. Ibid.

144. Ibid.

145. Ronald C. Lewis and Man Keung Ho, "Social Work with Native Americans," _Social Work_, (September, 1975), p. 381.

146. Ibid. p. 381.

147. Ibid. p. 381.

148. Ibid. p. 379.

149. Rene A. Ruiz and Amado M. Padilla.
     "Counseling Latino's," Personnel and
     Guidance Journal, (March, 1977), p. 401-402.

150. Sonia Badillo Ghali. "Culture Sensitivity
     and the Puerto Rican Client," Social
     Casework, (October, 1977.) See also:
     Edward W. Christensen, "When Counseling
     Puerto Ricans." Personnel and Guidance
     Journal, (March, 1977).

151. Ibid.

152. Ibid.

153. Rene A. Ruiz and Amado M. Padilla.
     "Counseling Latino's," Personnel and
     Guidance Journal, (March, 1977).

154. Kal Wagenheim. Puerto Rico: A Profile,
     (New York: Praeger Publishers, 1970).

155. Rene A. Ruiz and Amado M. Padilla.
     "Counseling Latino's," Personnel and Guidance
     Journal, (March, 1977).

156. Kal Wagenheim. Puerto Rico: A Profile,
     (New York: Praeger Publisher, 1970).

157. Ibid.

158. Sonia Badillo Ghali. "Culture Sensitivity
     and the Puerto Rican Client," Social
     Casework, (October, 1977).

159. Melvin Delgado. "Social Work on the Puerto
     Rican Community," Social Casework,
     (February, 1974).

160. Edwardo D. Maldonaldo Sierra, Richard D.
     Trent and Roman Marida. "Neurosis and
     Traditional Family Beliefs in Puerto Rico,"
     International Journal of Social Psychiatry,
     Vol. 6, (1960).

161. Sonia Badillo Ghali. "Culture Sensitivity
     and the Puerto Rican Client," Social
     Casework, (October, 1977).

162. Kal Wagenheim, Puerto Rico: A profile,
     (New York: Praeger Publishers, 1970)

163. Sonia Badillo Ghali. "Culture Sensitivity
     and the Puerto Rican," Social Casework,
     (October, 1977).

164. Ibid. p. 462.

165. Ibid. p. 463.

166. Ibid. p. 463.

167. Ibid. p. 463.

168. Armando Morales. "The Impact of Class
     Discrimination and White Racism on the Mental
     Health of Mexican-Americans," In Hernandez-
     Haugh-Wagner (ed.), Chicanos: Social and
     Psychological Perspective, St. Louis:
     C. V. Mosby Company, 1967), p. 211.

169. Hugh Butts. "White Racism: Its Origin,
     Institutions and the Implication for
     Professional Practice in Mental Health,"
     International Journal of Psychiatry,
     Vol. 8, No. 6, (December, 1969), p. 918.

170. David R. Burgest. "Racism in Everyday
     Language and Social Work Jargon," Social
     Work, (July, 1973); See also: Ignacio
     Aquilar, "Initial Contacts with Mexican-
     Americans' Families," Social Work, (May,
     1972), Marta Sotomayor "Mexican-American
     Interaction with Social Systems," Social

Casework, ((May 1971), John D. Cormican,
"Linguistic Issues in Interviewing," Social
Casework, (March 1975), Sonia Badillo Ghali.
"Culture Sensitivity and the Puerto Rican
Client," Social Casework, Vol. 58, No. 3,
(October, 1977).

171. Ignacio Aquilar. "Initial Contacts with
Mexican-American Families," Social Work (May
1972), p. 69.

172. Alejandro Garcia. "The Chicano and Social
Work," Social Casework, (May, 1971),
p. 275.

173. Ignacio Aquilar. "Initial Contacts with
Mexican-Americans," Social Work, (May
1972) p. 69.

174. Ibid. p. 69.

175. Elena Gonzales. "The Role of Chicano Folk
Beliefs and Practices on Mental Health," in
Hernandez-Haugh-Wagner (ed.) Chicano:
Social and Psychological Perspective,
(St. Louis: C. V. Mosby Company, 1967),
p. 265.

176. Ibid. p. 266.

177. Ibid. p. 266.

178. Ibid. p. 267.

179. Faustina Ramierz Knoll. "Casework Services
with Mexican-Americans," Social Casework,
(May, 1971), p. 282.

180. Ibid. pp. 89-90.

181. Elena Gonzales. "The Role of Chicano Folk
Beliefs on Practices in Mental Health," in
Hernandez-Haugh-Wagner (ed.), Chicano:
Social and Psychological Perspective,
(St. Louis: C. V. Mosby Company, 1967), p. 2

Chapter V.

SOME CRITICAL COMMENTS ON SOCIAL STUDY, DIAGNOSIS AND THEORY

Social study, diagnosis and the theory-base of social casework must not be viewed as separate components from the therapeutic relationship even though they may appear to be different. Study, diagnosis, and theory link together in an inter-changeable fashion to form the basis for social casework intervention.

According to Florence Hollis, who defines the term social study in her book, Casework: A Psychosocial Therapy:

> In the social study - the shorter term commonly used to refer to the psycho-social study -- the caseworker collects the facts upon which the diagnosis will be based.[182]

She goes further to delineate the differences between social study and diagnosis:

> It is extremely important to be clear about the differences between study and diagnosis. Social study is client-centered. It is the process of obser-vation and classification of the facts observed with the purpose of serving as much information as is needed to under-stand the client and his problem and to guide treatment wisely.[183]

Richmond, a predecessor of Hollis, describes social study and diagnosis as the following:

> The effort to get the essential facts bearing upon a man's social difficul-ties has commonly been called an inves-tigation, but the term adopted here as a substitute, social diagnosis, has the

advantage that from the first step it fixes the mind on the casework upon the end in view.[184]

It is clear that a reciprocal relationship exists between social study and diagnosis. Social diagnosis is a major link to social study in that the data obtained from social histories are arranged in such a manner as to offer a prescription for social work intervention. Hollis puts it in the following way:

> Diagnosis...is an opinion -- professional opinion. It represents the thinking of the worker about the facts and will be strongly influenced by the frame of reference he uses to guide him in understanding this meaning.[185]

> Diagnosis in casework is undertaken to answer the question, 'how can this person be helped?' Its objective is the formation of treatment plans' content, aims, and procedures.[186]

Mary Richmond elaborates further on the concept of social diagnosis by stating:

> Social diagnosis...attempts to make as exact a definition as possible for the situation and the personality, that is, in relationship to the other human beings upon whom he, in any way, depends on or depends upon him and in relation also to the social institutions of his community.[187]

Elizabeth Meier in her article, "Social and Cultural Factors in Casework Diagnosis," states:

> The **raison d' etre** for the social study and the diagnosis in casework is to provide a sound basis for treatment.[188]

As we analyze the significance of diagnosis in

casework intervention, we will find that the basis of the caseworker's judgment for intervention is rooted in the combined study and diagnosis available. We will also find that the social diagnosis provides a frame of reference for applying specific techniques to therapy. Furthermore, a social diagnosis provides consistency and synthesis in the treatment process, alleviating the need for "trial and error." Therefore, the frame of reference for the treatment process based on the diagnosis is usually tied into a theory (combination of theories) rather than the worker's own intuition or judgment. According to Hollis:

> What he wants to learn will inevitably be influenced by his frame of reference, that is the theories he holds about causation of difficulties in social functioning and about casework treatment methods.[189]

The theory-base underlying the study of the social and psychological functioning of individuals must be looked at from a cultural perspective. The ethnic/racial and cultural components often undermine the generic approach. According to Elizabeth Meier:

> His perception (client) of the object world, organization of these perceptions into a meaningful whole, and judgment in choosing goals (all functions of the ego) are strongly influenced by the value of his culture and class.[190]

The above observation is also relevant for different Third World ethnic and racial groups within the American society. Needless to say, the variables of self-study and social diagnosis as outlined by social scientists do not address the unique racial, ethnic and cultural variables of People of Color. It is "fool-hearty" and "wishful thinking" to assume that the cultural component is **understood** in the psychosocial study and diagnosis dynamics with People of Color in America.

A final link to social study and diagnosis is theory. Theory is the frame of reference, assumptions and orientation that underline the social casework strategies. There are many perspectives of theory, and a few of them are as follows:

> Theory is used to describe a logical explanation of the interrelatedness of a set of facts that have been empirical, verified, or are capable of being verified.[191]

> A theory has been instituted when propositions are logically interrelated.[192]

> There is an internally consistent body of verified hypotheses.[193]

> There is a more or less verified explanation of observed facts orphenomena.[194]

> The relationship between facts or the process of ordering facts is presented in some meaningful way.[195]

> The explanation of some class of events is present.[196]

> Explanations are provided for the phenomena of practice.[197]

The following case illustration will highlight the obstacles and difficulties inherent in study, diagnosis and theory as they may relate to the uniqueness of race, ethnicity and culture:

> **(Brother enters office of white clinician.** He is 19 years old, comes from a

family of seven, the third oldest child. He is dressed in a long sleeved purple shirt with a ruffled front, sky blue knickers, black lace up knee boots, a brown double-breasted suede jacket, a black Don Juan hat with a purple edging, and a small gold ear-ring. And he is sharp!)

Brother: What it is, man!

(White clinician immediately jots down in notebook, 'Speaks in "word hash".')

W. C.: What seems to be your problem, Joe?

Bro: Well, you see, I was in love with this stone fox, but I just couldn't get my shit together. My shit was raggedy.

(W. C. pictures in his mind's eye, a stone -- that is, concrete -- fox, jots, 'Fetishism and pervasion. Also, has past history of diarrhea.')

W. C.: Yes, go on, boy.

Bro: See, last Friday the eagle flew, (and cut that boy shit out), so I took my hog down the boulevard 'cause I decided to get myself a new slave.

W. C. jots down, 'Claims to bird watch, and to have ridden a hog down the street in a metropolitan community en route to purchasing a slave.')

W. C.: (Whispers softly) This boy is definitely experiencing delusions!

Bro: Anyway, I ran into my old lady and she laid a nickle on me -- I bought this shirt I have on with it, come to think of it. Then me and my partner,

sweat, slid on over to his woman's
place to pick up a bag of weed for a
dime.

W. C.: (Whispers) a nickle for a
shirt? Sliding to someone's home?
Buying weeds? (Louder) Yes, I see.

Bro: See, I'm a bad mother, and I like
to hold down a corner every now and
then.

(W. C. quickly jots down, 'inferiority
complex, claims to be bad and unworthy.
Low self-esteem also claims to hold
down corners in already-secure positions. Also shows improper sex identification, as he believes that he is a
woman and, in addition, a mother.')

Bro: We just laid dead there 'till the
hawk kept doing a job on us.

(W. C. jots down, 'Hallucinates about
being deceased. Persecutory complex
centered around being repeatedly at-
tacked by a hawk.')[198]

In this illustrious case above we can readily see
the obstacles that race, language and culture may
present if the traditional theory-base is being
used. We find impressions of behavior, language,
dress and life style being based on the myths,
assumptions and stereotypes existing about Black
culture and Black life rather than realities of
the culture. Implicit in all of the social
theory constructs and concepts pertaining to
People of Color, there appears to be the premise
of blaming the victim and his culture for the
difficulties he/she faces. There is no indication whatsoever that there may be something wrong
with the institution and/or person delivering
services or that the assessment tool is inadequate.

A more appropriate label for social theory concepts, such as culturally deprived, should be
"culturally different"; "culturally disadvantaged" is "culturally dispossessed"; and "Black
self-hatred" is the effects of "Racism". In this
way, the concepts used reflect the authentic and
proper dynamics interpreted.

According to Turner, the three terms essential to
theory are concepts, facts and hypothesis. The
author goes on to say that concepts are:

> ...presented to have accuracy and pre-
> cision for clear and effective communi-
> cation between colleagues... Facts...
> are concepts that he empirically tes-
> ted; that is, they are observations
> that are and others can make about the
> concepts with which we deal.[199]

It can be concluded from the above that theory is
little more than the subjective assumptions of a
worker based on his/her life experiences. A
theory implies a systematic learned body of knowledge that characterizes human behavior and human
functioning. In regard to how theory emerges,
Turner writes:

> Theory emerges through the process in
> which facts are ordered in a meaningful
> way: That is, the relationship between
> facts is positioned through observa-
> tion, speculation, inspiration and ex-
> perience and as such relationships are
> observed and verified, theory is de-
> veloped. Theory thus looks for facts
> and searches for relationship between
> facts.[200]

The next question to ask is "What is the purpose
of theory?" That is, why do practitioners need
theory in the first place? One author puts it
this way:

When a practitioner looks at theory, his goal is not to develop and refine an intellectual structure by which he can understand and manage the complex array of facts encountered in one practice, so that the nature of intervention can be reduced and effects of such intervention predicted. The clinician's principal interest is the utility of theory; what can it tell me about this situation that will permit me to act effectively?[201]

Some of the other uses of theory are to accomplish the following:

Ability to "predict" outcomes.
Ability to explain.
Alleviation of guesswork and impressions.
Anticipation of future outcomes on some situations and speculation on unanticipated.
Ability to help explain, recognize and understand new situations.
Alleviation of new surprises.
Explaination of activities to others.
Ability to help recognize new situations and gaps in knowledge.
Doing away with self-blame and guilt.
Ability to give order to case material.
Sense of security to therapist.

In spite of the stated needs for **theory** as provided above, there are constant debates within the practice of social casework therapy as to the relevance and importance of theory. Much of this is centered around the unresolved debate as to exactly how theory emerges. Finally, there are social work clinicians who question the validity of social casework theory because there is no theory of social casework intervention that has emerged from social casework practice. All of the theories used by social casework clinicians are borrowed from other social science disciplines. There are clinicians who feel that the theory underlying social casework practice should emerge from the practice of social casework. On the other hand, there are practitioners who feel that theory is hindsight and justification rather than providing a frame of reference for intervention. Practitioners justify this assumption from studies that have demonstrated that the placebo effect of practice is authentic. Above all, studies have demonstrated that practitioners do not alter intervention strategies with clients based on schools of thought or training. As one author puts it:

> ...do our theories emerge from our own practice or do they serve as sympathetic **'post hoc'** explanations of our practice observations? If theory does emerge from practice, does this happen in a highly formalized way, or is there only a strong but unspecified connection, or indeed is there any connection at all?[202]

The questions and debate continue:

> Might it be that theory and practice are two separate but necessary components of our practice, that what we do in our clinical practice is not based on our identical bases but on an experimentally based framework not yet systematised? Or further, it is even possible that at this point in our history the question is not relevant, that we do not have either singularly or plurally an adequate theoretical base for practice?[203]

Social work at the turn of the twentieth century was primarily concerned with meeting the needs of the poor through charity organizations. This was an outgrowth of the old English approach of meeting the needs of the poor.[204] During the advent of the psychoanalytic theory on human behavior in

220

the twentieth century, social work practice was heavily influenced by this theory. The psychoanalytic theory stressed the role of the unconscious and the unresolved psychosexual fixation as the cause for social adjustment problems with individuals in society. It was the onset of the Depression in the thirties and the resultant poverty of middle-class America that resulted in a shift of the psychoanalytical model. Earlier, the victim was blamed for his poverty. At this point, social work practioners turned to other theoretical premises. As one author puts it:

> Psychoanalysis with its focus on fantasies, dreams, childhood history, defenses and anxiety did not appear to provide much help for the social worker whose goals were to curb poverty...or meet the economic, social and psychological needs of a whole tenement of welfare clients.[205]

The difference between social theory and scientific theory is that the theories underlying the applied sciences are more or less verifiable. As one source puts it:

> A scientific theory is expressed formally as a series of related statements which together explain a class of phenomena. Especially outside (applied) science, however, theory has had more causal usage as a tentative proposal or conjecture put forth in explanation of certain phenomena, a proposal which serves as a basis or argument of experimentation and is not expressed in the rigorous form required of scientific theory. In (applied) science such a tentative proposal would be called a hypothesis rather than a theory... for example, certain psychoanalytic theories have been little confirmed in experimental investigation. Yet, such theories have, nevertheless, been found

useful as a basis for clinical work and as a source of new perspective on human behavior.[206]

As stated earlier, the primary purpose of diagnosis is to plan intervention strategies. Brair and
Miller in their book, Problems and Issues in Social Casework, suggest three uses for diagnosis.
The first is classification and categorization,
such as employing typologies of **neurotic, psycho-
tic, character disorder** and **multi-problems**,
while the other usage refers to the understanding
of the dynamics that may be called the **verstehn**
concept of diagnosis, and the third type is referred to as a process or procedure followed by
the worker in order to continue the case. In con-
structing a diagnostic typology, one author
points out:

> The central assumption of this approach
> is that if one can group similar cases
> together, he will be able to develop an
> intervention strategy specific to that
> type of case; moreover, if a common
> etiology can be discovered for a group
> of cases, it may be possible to devise
> a method of intervention directed to
> causes rather than symptoms.[207]

Thus, the social study and diagnosis as a method
of planning intervention is based on a theory, a
hunch and/or a conjecture about the interrelated-
ness of facts and what should be done.

In spite of the fact that the diagnosis in social
casework includes: (1) the individuals, interpersonal factors and his/her lcoation in the
social network, (2) interpersonal systems or the
interaction units (dyads, triads), (3) the family
unit as a social system and (4) the family unit's
interchange within its social network, the unique
racial and ethnic component is usually overlooked
and ignored.

In any scientific research there is always the

222

underlying question of control for biases in the research question, design and/or procedure. There are those who hold the position that there is no such thing as freedom from control of cultural biases because the questions and hypotheses being contemplated by the researcher are derived from a bias. On the other hand, there is a school of thought that supports the view that cultural biases exist but can be controlled in the research design and format. Given the origin of social theory that is somewhat different from scientific rigorous research, it is easy to see how prejudices and biases can become incorporated in a body of knowledge. We can see the potential for self-fulling prophesies and the use of theory to cover up and camouflage inadequacies, prejudices and racism in regard to minorities.

The fact of the matter is that there are few, if any, social theories utilized by social caseworkers that have been derived from a racial, ethnic and cultural context. This is not to say that there are not theories that have not addressed themselves to the total person as well as the internal and external development of individual and groups; however, such generic theories, which include minorities and nonminorities alike, do not incorporate the cultural components and reactions necessary. In addition, many of the negative external environmental forces affecting People of Color do not exist for nonminorities.

This is not to suggest that Caucasian social work practitioners and theorists are automatically prejudiced and biased (just because they are white) in their attitudes toward minority cultures. However, the application of white middle-class Western concepts and constructs onto racial and ethnic minorities results in inappropriate classifications and categorizations of Third World behavior. Consequently, there emerged such views of People of Color as:

    Viewing People of Color as innately in-

ferior due to their uncouth
and "uncivilized behavior" (prior to
the 1920's).

Viewing lack of motivation, lack of
self-discipline and inability to delay
gratification as the source of Third
World ignorance, inferiority and poverty.
(1920 - 40's).

Viewing the effects of discrimination
and segregation as the cause for lack of
motivation and uncouth and uncivilized
behavior (1950's).

Viewing the structure and pathology of
the Black family as responsible for the
ignorance and inferiority of the Black family.
(1960's).

Viewing Black "self-hatred" as the
cause for all the social ills of the
Black and Third World community, such
as lack of motivation, uncouth and uncivilized behavior (1980's).

If we were to analyze these hypotheses closely,
we would find that the underlying assumptions of
Black and minority behavior have not changed
since the Europeans' first contact with Africans;
only the labels have changed. Many ethnic minorities are still looked at as being backward,
stupid, ignorant and uncivilized, but the labels
have changed from innately inferior, poverty,
discriminate and "Black self-hatred." As the
social theorists went into the Black and minority
communities of the late 1950's and early 1960's
with (possible) honest intentions, but with
instruments based on white culture and norms,
they emerged with such prevalent theoretical
concepts of the Black and minority communities
as:

Culturally deprived: Blacks and other
minorities do not have a culture,

224

and/or if they do, it is inadequate and inappropriate.

Culturally disadvantaged: The Black and minority cultures are inferior.

Hardcore: The cultures of these individuals are pathological and untreatable.

Hard-to-reach: The minority members do not respond adequately to the techniques and therapy available to them.

Deprived: Minorities lack the internal and external ingredients to function adequately.

Disadvantaged: Minorities lack the appropriate commodities inherent in white society to function adequately.

High risk: Minorities are incapable of responding effectively to the therapeutic tools available.

Underpriviledged: Same as disadvantaged.

Black self-hatred: It is Black and other minority hate of self because they are not white that is responsible for the difficulties.

Cultural lag: There is an inability of members in the minority culture to seek and respond favorably to the institutions available in their community for help.

One of the major difficulties with Western-oriented social theories as a tool for analyzing behavior of People of Color rest with the differences in the philosophical assumptions of the Western world view and Eastern world view. The theoretical assumptions regarding behavior and interaction of Europeans and Western man may be antithetical to ethnic and racial minorities of the Eastern epistemological world view. However, the following assumptions, which underline the philosophical orientation for Western therapy, are in opposition to the Eastern world view. Some of the underlying assumptions of the Western oriented world view as opposed to the Eastern world view are as follows:

Survival of the fittest is the rule vs. group cohesion.

Only internal and external forces are the causes of man's psychological skills as opposed to supernatural causes.

Highest value is placed on individualism as opposed to cooperativeness.

Self-preservation is the first law of nature as opposed to collective behavior.

Democracy is ideal for all, as opposed to socialism or some other form of government.

Protestant work ethic is supreme.

Man is driven by the self-pleasure principle as opposed to major concern for others.

Man is driven by positive and negative reinforcement from within his/her environment as opposed to being driven by a Supreme Being.

Man-made laws are supreme (until changed) as opposed to the laws of a Supreme Being having priority.

The deficits in social casework theory may be summed up in the following manner:

> No theories of casework sufficiently address the unique racial and cultural variables that may serve as a stimulus to behavior.

> No theories of social casework sufficiently address the impact of overt and covert racism in the psyche of minorities (who live in a hostile environment).

> No theories of social casework have sufficiently addressed the side effects of racism and prejudice upon the psyche of the white individual or group.

> No theory of social casework practice has systematised the knowledge-base on the dynamics involved when worker/client is of a different or same racial/ethnic group.

> No theory of social casework has done away with the ethnocentric view of Western philosophy or has sufficiently incorporated the practices and beliefs of minority groups.

In analyzing any theory for social casework practices, the therapist must consider the following:

> The unique racial/ethnic and cultural variables that may serve as stimulus for behavior.

> Impact and effects of racism upon the white individual and group psyche.

> The impact of ethnic/racial differences on the worker/client relationship.

> The epistemological world view of the

ethnic/racial minority concerned.

The psycho-historical perspective on the environment and culture of minority clients.

182. Florence Hollis. Casework: A Psychosocial Therapy, (New York: Random House, 1964), pp. 169-170.

183. Ibid. p. 170.

184. Mary Richmond. Social Diagnosis, (New York: The Free Press, 1917), p. 26.

185. Florence Hollis. Casework: A Psychosocial Therapy, (New York: Random House, 1964), p. 178.

186. Ibid. p. 178.

187. Mary Richmond. Social Diagnosis, p. 51.

188. Elizabeth Meier. "Social and Cultural Factors in Casework Diagnosis," Social Work, (July, 1959), p. 15.

189. Ibid. p. 16.

190. Ibid. p. 16.

191. Robert K. Merton, Social Theory and Social Structure, (New York: The Free Press. 1968).

192. Ibid.

193. Ibid.

194. Gordon Hearn, "General Systems Theory and Social Work," in Social Work Treatment: Interlocking Theoretical Approaches, (New York: The Free Press, 1979).

195. William J. Goode and Paul K. Hath, Methods in Social Research, (New York: McGraw-Hill. 1952).

196. Alfred L. Baldwin. Theories of Child Development, (New York: Wiley, 1980).

197. Harold Lewis. "Practice Science and
     Professional Development: Responsive to New
     Knowledge and Values," Symposium on the
     Effectiveness of Social Work Intervention:
     Implication for Curriculum Change, (New York:
     Fordman University, 1971).

198. Alan K. Meason. "The Black Man's Burden:
     The White Clinician," The Black Scholar,
     (July-August, 1975), pp. 15-16.

199. Frances J. Turner. Social Work Treatment
     Interlocking Theoretical Approaches, (New
     York: The Free Press, 1979), p. 2.

200. Ibid. p. 1.

201. Ibid. p. 8.

202. Ibid. p. 1

203. Ibid. p. 1

204. Frances J. Turner. Social Work Treatment
     Interlocking Theoretical Approaches, (New
     York: The Free Press, 1979), pp. 2-3.

205. Herbert S. Strean, Social Casework:
     Theories in Action, (Metuchen: The Scarecrow
     Press, Inc., 1971), p. 5.

206. Ibid. p. 5.

207. Scott Brair and Henry Miller. Problems and
     Issues in Social Casework, (New York:
     Columbia University Press, 1971), p. 147.

Davis, Ossie, 45n

Delgado, Melvin, 209n,

Diagnosis:
  defined, 213

E

Eastern world view:
  description, xv;
  origin of, 51-52;
  history, 52-55;
  relevance to social
  casework, 56-58

Epistemology:
  defined, xvii

Ethnicity:
  defined, xv,

F

Fanon, Frantz, 67, 84n

Fibush, Esther, 45n,
158n

Fischer, Newell, 159n

Freedom from
Prejudices, 13-14

Freud, Sigmund, 69, 84n

Fromm-Reichmann, R.,
  85n

Frye, Charles, 53, 82n

Garcia, Alejandro, 211n

Gardner, LaMaurice H.,
  160n, 161n

Ghali, Sonia Badillo,
  46n, 209n, 210n, 211n

Gitterman, Alex, 83n,
  158n

Gochros, Jean S., 88,
  84n, 158n

Gonzales, Elena, 81n,
  211n

Goode, William J., 229n

Good Tracks, Jimm G.,
  224n

Greenson, R., 69, 85n

Grier, William H.,
  159n, 160n, 161n,
  162n

H

Hath, Paul K., 229n

Strean, Herbert S.,
230n

Study, diagnosis,
theory: defined,
212-215; deficits,
217-219; case
illustration,
216-217;
interpretation, 219-
226; role of worker
in practice,227

Sue, Derald Wing, 84n,

Sue, Stanley, 84n

Sullivan, H. S., 85n

Szasa, T., 84n, 85n

T

Third World
Minorities: defined,
xv

Transference: defined,
69-70; analysis of,
70-72; Black/white
interaction, 73-76;
variables affecting,
77-80

Transference/
Countertransference:
sexuality, 115-118

Trent, Richard D.,
210n

Turner, Frances J.,
210n

V

Vontress, Clemmont E.,
83n, 86n

W

Wagenheim, Kal, 209n,
210n

White and whiteness:
defined, 18

White, Jessie A., 81n

White, R. W., 85n

White worker/Black
client relationship:
97-98, 102-103, 108-
109; role of worker,
87, 114-115, 130-
131;; case
illustrations, 88-90,
95-96, 98-100, 104-
106, 109-110, 110-111

Woodson, Carter G.,
159n

Y

Yabura, Lloyd, 46n

Brief Biographical Sketch

Mwalimu David R. Burgest is a graduate of Paine College (B.A.), Wayne State University (M.S.W.) and Syracuse University (Ph.D.). He is the recipient of many awards and certificates in social work and community services. He has been affiliated with the field of social work for the past twenty years as practitioner, educattor, consultant and volunteer. He has taught at Syracuse University School of Social Work as Assistant Professor; Associate Professor of Psychology at Upstate Medical Center (State of New York) Cooperative College; Visiting Professor of Sociology and Coordinator of Field Placement at the University of Nairobi in Nairobi, Kenya (East Africa) and University Professor of Social Work at Governors State University in University Park, Illinois.

Mwalimu David R. Burgest has presented numerous papers and coordinated workshops widely in the United States, Europe and Africa. Dr. Burgest's publications have appeared in such journals as Social Work, Black Scholar, Western Journal of Black Studies, Black Books Bulletin, Black Caucus, Journal of Black Studies and Black Male/Female Relationship Journal. He is the author and editor of one book entitled Social Work Practice with Minorities, Scarecrow Press, 1982.

Mwalimu Burgest is married to the former Loretta Jean Black and is the father of four children: Juanita Marie, Angela Lynore, David Raymond II and Paul Reginald.